To Shirley

Thank you for the last 30 years, for your support, love and trust.

Thank you for helping me fulfil my dreams, and more than anything,
thank you for being there when I needed you most.

I have come to realise that you can only truly value something when you've lost it.

Lots of love Peter.

So much of this life is an illusion.

RECIPES FOR Life

I used to think I was invincible...

...Then I was told I had a tumour the size of a satsuma growing in my bowel. Suddenly the world as I knew it came to a grinding halt. Cancer was about to launch me into a different stratosphere. I had no idea how much my life, and everything I valued, was about to change.

Before my diagnosis I was what is politely called 'driven.' I didn't stop to consider what I had. I constantly pushed myself on, trying to do better, to earn more. I worked day and night building my publishing company. I had a staff of 28. I travelled the world and ate meals fashioned by top chefs at the world's leading restaurants.

At the time I thought life was pretty good. Then the doctor told me what was growing in my bowel. It's funny but none of that materialistic stuff has mattered to me since.

Being told I had cancer made me feel two things: the first being shock. I couldn't have been more surprised. I suppose no one expects to be told they have cancer but I didn't even feel ill. I wasn't old either, I was 51. I had had grumbling pains in my abdomen but my doctor had said it was diverticulitis – something many men my age get.

The second thing I felt was anger. I was cross that cancer could come and mess up my world like this. I left the clinic after receiving my diagnosis feeling utterly furious at this disease. I got in my car and zoomed off and inevitably, given the way I was driving during the journey home, I was stopped for speeding. After finding out what I had gone through that day the kindly policeman decided to let me off. It was one of the few good things to happen to me during that time.

Initially I was in denial that this was really happening to me. I tried to carry on as normal with plans to open a delicatessen and a restaurant. I refused to accept that this was going to interrupt my life at all. I carried on working as to have stopped would have been to acknowledge the cancer. However, I soon discovered that carrying on as normal wasn't going to be possible.

I was very upfront with everyone that I had cancer. Then I found out that people treat you very differently when you have cancer. People backed away from me, they were not as easy in my company, they were more reserved. Some long standing clients lost confidence in me, some clients, who I now count as true friends, said 'forget the job, get better and we will start the project when you return.'

How could I suddenly be so changed to so many people? For me, it was among the most shocking revelations about life with the Big C.

And there were plenty of other shocks in store. Within three weeks of my diagnosis I was having surgery to remove the tumour along with 9 inches of my bowel. It certainly wasn't something I had planned for in my diary. Life with cancer is about dealing with surprises.

Everything became a question of percentages. I was told that if there were between four and 10 cancer cells left outside of my bowel then there would be a 50% chance that it would kill me. If I had chemotherapy then it would be six months of hell but then it would improve my chances by 15%. Or I could have six months of pure recklessness knowing that soon I was going to die. As I toyed with my options, I started thinking of things to do before my time was up.

In the end I went for chemotherapy. I had eight months of it from November until May. I had private health insurance so had the luxury of utilising the facilities at Leaders in Oncology Care (more of which you can read about on the following pages) where the care I was given was amazing.

Yet private treatment or not, the disease you are fighting is the same. I used to look at the people in the cubicles next to me also receiving their infusions of drugs. I knew the statistics: one in three of us having treatment wouldn't make it. I would count along three cubicles – one, two, which one of that three would it be – me?

It might save your life but chemo is no fun. Chemo brain struck very quickly. Suddenly my short term memory was shot to pieces. My mouth became full of ulcers. Everyone is different but I didn't want to have to worry about social niceties when I had beating cancer to worry about, or cause loved ones to have to see me suffer. Stupid plan really but I did some stupid things. So I stayed by myself in my little flat and worried only about offending myself. I had to go home once: I had never suffered from migraines before but when one struck I needed support, so I called Shirley and she was there for me. Thank God. ▶

Most days when I woke up in my bed feeling thoughtful, I used to picture myself balancing on the end of a plank and if I fell off I was not going to make it and if I didn't fall off I would be OK. Come what may I did not want to give in and fall off that plank.

Months went by and finally I was told what I had wanted to hear ever since my diagnosis: I was in remission. As anyone who has been in my position will know it's not a question of: 'phew now that cancer has gone, let's get back to life again.' I was a different person and, as odd as it may sound, coming out of that treatment was a difficult transition. Going for chemotherapy had been a comforting routine in my crazy world. When you are going through the treatment there are lots of people who look after you, who check how you are. Then suddenly you are on your own again with no chemo to hide behind. Instead of excited I felt that I was once again exposed to the cold and brutal world. I felt vulnerable.

Doctors who treat people with cancer talk about a window of opportunity. This typically hits six weeks or so after treatment when cancer patients feel inspired to change their habits and their lives for the better.

My window really hit hard. I felt as if I had been given this opportunity to change my life and to have one more go at it.

I realised I didn't want things to be so unrelenting. I was working incredibly hard just to pay the monthly wage bill. I decided to downsize my business and I cut my staff from 28 to 4. Some clients stayed with me – some decided not to. This was fine because – well, it's a bit of a cliché, but cancer helped me sort out what was important to me. Before I used to love fashion, nice cars, flash watches, jewels but suddenly none of that appealed to me – and it was really, really quite nice.

I also wanted to safeguard my health more. I wanted to eat better. I wanted to learn how I should be eating.

Before, I didn't think about what I ate – I didn't even really acknowledge that there is anything that you can class as unhealthy food.

This is where the idea for this book was born. How should people who have, or have had, cancer eat? I had no idea.

It was also a chance for me to give something back to those people who helped me while I underwent chemotherapy at the LOC and to give something to those people who will have cancer in the future.

Having forged a career based in the restaurant trade, food has always been a special part of my life and so a book of recipes seemed a natural way for me to do this.

To do this book I needed new recipes and help from the experts. I spoke with Michel Roux, who has become a great friend and supporter, and he wrote to a few chefs he knew, I also contacted some chefs I also knew, and the response was amazing. We asked chefs who, like me, had been touched personally somehow by cancer, and every single one of them agreed to help by devising and contributing their own recipes, and the book was born.

Seeing this book completed is one of the most satisfying highs of my career, and I have quite a few to choose from. I hope it helps inspire people to eat better. As I have discovered, nourishing food need not be virtuous and dull – it can be alluring and delicious as can be seen from these recipes.

I am delighted that half the income from this book will go towards the Living Well programme of the LOC. As you can read in more detail further on, the ethos of the centre is to support people through cancer and help them through the jolt back to the real world. They also work on the windows to help people make their new life a healthier life.

If it helps just one cancer survivor improve the quality of their life then I will feel as if I have achieved something.

Cancer can be a life ruiner there's no doubt about that. But I am taking my chance to start life over again and running with it – in some cases literally. I have taken up sports and play badminton four times a week. I have suffered my first sports injury at the age of 53.

Yes I am eating better. Many of the recipes from this book are now favourites of mine – like the Camargue rice – it really is delicious.

I have been lucky enough to survive cancer. I have been given that chance to start again and I am going to take it. In some ways you could argue that my window of opportunity is still open.

I hope that this book inspires others to feel the same way I do.

September 2013

Peter Marshall

Acknowledgements

To Michel Roux, for being such a good friend and who was such a good help in ensuring I got the best care and for being there whenever a good friend was needed.

To all the chefs, for giving up their time and for their menu creations, ensuring we have published a unique book that I hope will help many people.

To Kelly, who has been an amazing support in the production of this book and really is a true gem.

To Dr Slevin and his team of wonderful nurses, who ensured I got through the difficult times of chemotherapy.

To the doctors and nurses at the Chiltern Hospital, when they first looked after me and ensured a successful operation.

To Robert and Wendy for being good friends.

To Olivia, my very stoic PA who put up with all my tantrums and mood swings and for helping me organise this book. To Philip, who I have worked with for 20 years and who made sure that this book was designed to a truly high standard, and to Helen, for making sure that all the words were correct.

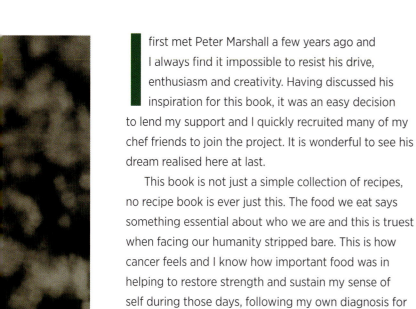

I first met Peter Marshall a few years ago and I always find it impossible to resist his drive, enthusiasm and creativity. Having discussed his inspiration for this book, it was an easy decision to lend my support and I quickly recruited many of my chef friends to join the project. It is wonderful to see his dream realised here at last.

This book is not just a simple collection of recipes, no recipe book is ever just this. The food we eat says something essential about who we are and this is truest when facing our humanity stripped bare. This is how cancer feels and I know how important food was in helping to restore strength and sustain my sense of self during those days, following my own diagnosis for rectal cancer.

I was very fortunate that after an initial successful operation carried out by Professor John Northover, my treatment was expertly supervised by Dr Slevin and his marvellous team at the London Oncology Clinic. This remarkable place became my world for six months whilst undergoing fortnightly intensive chemotherapy sessions, a cocoon I could trust with complete confidence. I can gratefully and humbly say that after seven years since first diagnosis, I am fully recovered and healthy; for this I credit also my precious family and friends whose support was immense.

The book provides a crucial reference for young and old alike, whose lives are affected by the fight against cancer. It is not a set of rules, there are no diktats here, just simple pleasurable food with integrity.

No unreasonably demanding or complicated dish has found its way into this collection, all the recipes can be prepared and eaten in real life at home rather than an abstract, professional kitchen. I urge you to use your instinct and combine with our inspiration to let your true desires guide you.

I am proud to share these pages with friends and fellow chefs all of whom I respect and admire and whose lives, like mine and Peter's, have been touched by cancer in some way. Together we share the same passion to inspire and invigorate.

Food is life, it is positive, life giving, nurturing and nourishing. It is often all you think about when you are recovering from the latest round of treatment and fantasising about the perfect meal. Food is love, it is an embrace and offers hope; every carer knows the powerful, positive feeling of giving nourishment, each spoonful imbued with love, optimism and strength.

I learned a momentous lesson during my months of treatment, the importance of moderation, balance and good quality, light, fresh food packed with nutrients. Since appetites and meals tend to be small, each morsel must count and pack a punch, both in terms of taste and nutrition. We all wish to maintain our health and know that prevention is better than cure; these recipes assist this endeavour. Here you will find tempting treats and healthy food ideas, a book that lifts the spirits.

To eat is to live and this book provides powerful, pure pleasure and inspiration.

Michel Roux, OBE

Dr Maurice Slevin

M
ost of us will find our lives touched by cancer in some way, be it via a casual acquaintance, or a close loved one who has the disease.

Thankfully, though, few of us have to confront the life and death nature of cancer on a daily basis.

Yet Dr Maurice Slevin and his staff at Leaders in Oncology Care (LOC) have to do just that.

On a typical day forty or so patients will be in the treatment room watching TV, playing about on-line or just reading a book as they receive their own special cocktail of chemotherapy drugs. Others will be upstairs in the consulting rooms talking to their doctors. Some will be at the beginning of their chemotherapy journey and adjusting to what lies ahead of them. Others will be about to step back into their life to start again without cancer.

Some will be receiving news that is very hard for them to confront. Their doctors must carefully choose their words to explain that a cure is not something they can promise any more.

'Increasingly these days many people can be 'cured' of their cancer but you can't always 'cure' them. Even if you can't 'cure' their cancer you can frequently prolong their life and improve the quality of their life,' says Dr Slevin.

Dr Slevin, an oncologist with three decades experience, admits that working so closely with life and death issues inevitably makes him question his own mortality from time to time. However, it also makes him highly sensitive not just to the physical needs of a cancer patient, but their emotional needs too.

'Our aim is to take the difficult situation that our patients are in and to make it as bearable as possible,' he says.

'Everything about this clinic has been designed especially for cancer patients – they are its entire focus.'

Now occupying two large buildings on Harley Street the LOC is nothing like you might expect a cancer clinic to feel. The overriding atmosphere is calm and reassuring: it is anything but austere or clinical. The walls are dotted with ocean scenes and sky shots. The staff smile easily.

Dr Slevin founded LOC with three colleagues back in 2005 and is understandably proud of what has been achieved there.

Leading figures from the National Health Service and from healthcare centres from around the world come to visit LOC to gain inspiration for their own clinics and hospitals.

There are now over 70 consultants working there. Like Dr Slevin, who specialises in the treatment of breast, lung, ovarian and gastro intestinal cancers, many of the other consultants are also leaders in their field.

Numerous patients owe their life to the clinic's high standards of care. Yet its success lies not just in the medicine.

'The philosophy of the LOC is very much that having and treating cancer is not just a case of getting drugs or having that operation: it is about allowing people to be in control of their lives,' says Dr Slevin.

'We want them to feel looked after and confident.

'So we have the optimal environment and chose staff with the right approach and the right attitude to ensure it is well staffed and that people have the care and support they need.'

Dr Slevin began practising oncology in the National Health Service at St Bartholomew's Hospital in London, but became frustrated that he couldn't always do as much for his patients there as he wanted to. It was this frustration that led him to start a private practice and ultimately to set up the LOC.

'Over time I began to realise that in doing private practice I was able to practice oncology without the inevitable restrictions that are created by the National Health Service,' he says.

'In private practice I liked the fact that I could give people all the drugs they needed without being told it was too expensive and I could get investigations done for people within a very short period of time. It became to me a very attractive way of practising' he explains.

However although the LOC is a private practice the idea was to set a high benchmark of care that would improve standards elsewhere too. He is 'delighted' that much of what they have done at the LOC is being replicated within the NHS. As Dr Slevin says: 'Cancer can affect anyone.

'Many people from the top echelons of the National Health Service come here to see what we do and how we do it,' he says.

'Also the majority of our consultants also work in the NHS and so they take their experience of working here with us with them'.

Dr Slevin who has published over 200 medical papers and has sat on many research based committees is always keen to take advantage of the latest breakthroughs to help his patients.

'That's one of the things that appealed to me about specialising in oncology – the fact that the treatment of cancer is intellectually challenging.

'There are new things happening all the time,' he says. 'Yet what I also enjoy about it is the fact that when you treat someone for cancer you see them for a long period of time so that really get to know them. You also get a chance to really make a difference to someone's life.'

To ensure patients at the LOC receive the treatment most likely to succeed for them they have implemented a state of the art information technology system so that they can see which doctors are using which treatments and which ones have the best outcome. It also means that all the doctors can refer to various scientific data to help them when they are deciding on which drugs to use.

'So for example if someone needs anti-sickness medication we use the one that has the best possible effect,' explains Dr Slevin proudly.

Improving the quality of life for patients has been something of a life mission for him. In 1985, for example, he helped found CancerBACUP, one of the first charities to offer support and information from both cancer patients and their families.

'Cancer affects people in many different ways and the idea was to bring emotional support,' says Dr Slevin.

It's because he believes in this holistic approach to helping people with cancer that he was happy for the LOC to be associated with this book.

'Good nutrition is helpful for anyone with a serious illness but it is especially important to eat a well-balanced healthy diet to support your body when undergoing cancer treatment.'

LOC
Leaders in Oncology Care

Kelly McCabe

The expert advice

Take a few quality ingredients and a few basic cooking skills and just about anyone can put together a tasty meal.

Yet putting together a meal that not only tastes delicious but is also good for you is far more of a challenge. Knowing what to eat after a cancer diagnosis can be a confusing and conflicting subject.

That's why we asked the LOC specialist oncology dietician Kelly McCabe to help advise the chefs who took the time to develop recipes for this book. Kelly could guide them, with her expertise in the nutritional requirements of people following cancer treatment, about the best ingredients and cooking methods to use to help improve the nutritional quality of each and every dish in this book.

'I think this book is a really important project because patients are always asking what they can and can't or should and shouldn't eat,' says Kelly.

'Unfortunately, evidence-based answers to such questions are often difficult to find. A lot of diets aimed at people with cancer are restrictive, focus on foods you should cut out and are not based on scientific research'.

'What I like about this book is that it is focussing on great tasting food that is also good for you and presents the science in a simple, practical way.

'I was really impressed by how seriously the chefs took the challenge. The meals they have developed are suitable not just for those who have completed cancer treatment but also for those simply trying to eat well to improve their health.'

Diet alone is not going to prevent or cure cancer. However, a healthy diet is part of an overall lifestyle that can help to reduce the risk of cancer.

Kelly offers tips throughout the book to show people how making small changes can have a big impact on their overall diet. She wants to demystify healthy eating.

'There are some simple swaps that can help improve your diet without leaving you feeling deprived,' she says.

'For example, from time to time why not have venison rather than beef as venison is still a good source of iron and protein is lower in saturated fat than beef.

'Rather than a standard white potato you could try having sweet potato which has a low glycaemic index (meaning it provides a slow release of energy rather than a quick burst of energy followed by a slump) and is also a good source of vitamin A.

Just including foods with a variety of colours into your meals – such as yellow peppers alongside red tomatoes helps ensure a diversity of nutrients.'

Kelly hopes that the book will help to inspire cancer patients and their families' to eat well but also to enjoy their food: 'after all,' she says. 'Eating should be a shared experience – something that is enjoyed - a pleasure.

I met Peter Marshall only recently and we sat and talked in my garden in Esher for two solid hours. I was fascinated by his deep knowledge of the people and stars who represent our industry. Since our meeting I have formed an opinion in my mind of a man dedicated to creating a moving picture of all that is good in food in restaurants and hotels. In other words, an apothecary of excellence.

In contrast, I first met Michel Roux in the mid seventies at a launch party for a BBC food programme. Even then, he was held in high esteem by all chefs and by the public. I am delighted that the name Roux has become iconic and that he and his brother Albert are the patriarchs of a rising dynasty. The three of us have now become 'statistics' of this particular illness and this enables us to speak from the heart.

In this inspired book you will find some glorious, simple and not so simple recipes from some wonderful chefs like John Williams and Andrew Fairlie and my old young friends Steve Drake and Jason Atherton amongst many others.

I have no research laboratory to conduct experiments so cannot really speak on the basis of scientific facts; all I have is some experience based on my age and lessons learnt from life's many obstacles.

The sourcing of good ingredients and cooking them in as simple a way as possible will always be a signpost for healthy eating. Progress has thrown up some new super food candidates such as beetroot, avocado, mango and pomegranates and spices such as turmeric.

One pot meals eliminate complications and give a wholesome result. A French classic, poulet grandmère, is a good example. In a 'Le Creuset' type casserole, brown some chicken pieces, then add chopped shallots, garlic, potatoes and mushrooms. Cover in chicken stock and bake in the oven. My present favourite is steamed cod with lemon and pure Cretan olive oil to which you can add diced skinned tomatoes and parsley. One has also to remember that over-grilling and over-charring can be less than healthy.

Also over-fiddling and over-processing ingredients will remove any benefits. These days beetroot appears cooked every which way. My mother used to marinate the cooked beet in oil and vinegar and serve it sliced with garlic mayonnaise. Delicious and simple. I also recall one of the dishes Michel Roux served us in St Tropez; a frisée salad with aromas of garlic and hints of truffle with chunks of garlic bread and quite heavily laced with vinegar, which is Michel's hallmark in the dressing of salads. We also find ourselves at home eating soups in different guises.

Having said all this, in the words of Peter Marshall "after a session of chemotherapy all you want is a juicy steak or a piece of chocolate". Anything, in moderation, that makes you happy is a good thing. The recipes in this book have been created by highly knowledgeable chefs and they point the way forward towards healthier and more balanced eating which should help reduce any risks.

Good luck and bon appétit!

Nico Ladenis

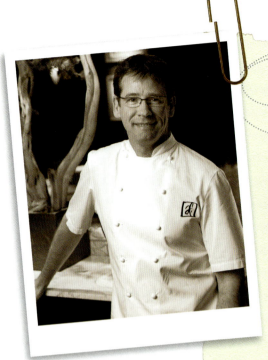

Andrew Fairlie

At fifteen, Andrew began a classical four-year apprenticeship in his hometown of Perth. By the age of twenty, he became the first recipient of the prestigious Roux Scholarship and remains to this day its youngest scholar. Andrew further cemented his relationship with the Scholarship by joining the prestigious judging panel in 2006.

The Roux scholarship presented an unprecedented honour for a British chef – to work in the kitchen of Michael Guerard, one of the great masters of French culinary tradition. Guerard's approach to cooking was inspirational and Andrew still adheres to his mentor's ethos of 'simple food, brilliantly done'.

After more than two years in France, Andrew spent two seasons aboard the luxurious 5-star Royal Scotsman train, before journeying south to the Ritz Hotel in London to take up the position of senior Sous chef.

Andrew returned to his native Scotland in 1995 to become executive chef at Glasgow's One Devonshire Gardens Hotel and received not only acceptance into the esteemed Royal Academy of Culinary Arts but also his first Michelin star which he held till his departure in 2001.

2001 saw the opening of Andrew's eponymous restaurant within the heart of the legendary Gleneagles Hotel. Within its first year the restaurant was awarded a Michelin star followed by a stream of awards.

In 2005 Andrew was tasked with cooking both a state banquet and the dinner for Her Majesty The Queen and more good news was to follow when Restaurant Andrew Fairlie was awarded its second Michelin Star, the first and only two star restaurant in Scotland.

The pinnacle of Andrews career was to be awarded to him in Lisbon 2011 when he was given the title of Grande Chef du Monde by Relais & Châteaux. He joins a list of only 160 of the best chefs in the world to hold this honour.

CHEF'S VIEW

"Although there are many, many books written on healthy eating, some of which are very good and many more which are very bland and boring, I think this book is very different for many reasons. First of all it addresses the relationship between food and a specific disease, a disease that everyone at some point in their lifetime will be affected by either directly or indirectly.

Speaking from personal experience I truly believe that what we consume has a major effect on the healing process both physically and mentally. It has inspired some of the country's best chefs to get involved and create recipes that are simple, creative and healthy. It has also inspired chefs to think about the health benefits of food and I know they have found it both challenging and rewarding in equal measures. It provides recipes that can be enjoyed by the whole family which I think is tremendously important as it keeps family meal times as normal as they can be, and to that end everyone can enjoy the benefits of healthy eating which can only be a positive."

Daniel Galmiche

Born in Lure in the Comte region of Eastern France, Daniel was enthralled with cooking from an early age. After leaving school, he took up a three year apprenticeship with Chef Yves Lalloz, who ran a fine restaurant with a farm attached enabling Daniel to work with ingredients from the field to the plate.

His career has taken him all over the world including Sweden, Portugal and Singapore. In London he worked at the highly acclaimed Le Gavroche under the tutelage of Michel Roux as well as achieveing a Michelin star at Harvey's in Bristol, maintaining a Michelin star at L'Ortolan near Reading and regaining a Michelin star at the magnificent Cliveden House in Berkshire.

Today, Daniel is Executive Head Chef at the Vineyard at Stockcross in Berkshire, he regularly appears on regional and national television and has cooked for many famous celebrities including Jude Law and Pierce Brosnan.

CHEF'S VIEW

"Peter contacted me on Michel Roux Snr's suggestion that I should get involved in this book. My wife had breast cancer 8 years ago and to me it made sense to contribute to this book as I have lived with the disease as well as cooking with it.

My Italian wife could not eat dairy and cheese and meat, which of course is prominent in an Italian diet and to make it easier I said I would eat the same as her. Now we eat this way all the time, always with olive oil and only a little butter as a rule, but always natural, fresh, home cooked food that is seasonal. Now it comes naturally to me to cook this way and it can be seen on the menu at The Vineyard too. My customers often remark that the dishes served are very light and natural, which of course is unusual for a Frenchman as traditional French food can be quite "heavy" with lots of cream and full fat milk.

I have found putting these recipes together an interesting learning curve and think that this book as a whole will be very useful to a lot of people and hopefully they will know that by creating this book and the recipes in it that we are thinking about them."

Galton Blackiston

Galton left school at 17 to play cricket professionally, but was not quite good enough to pursue as a career. As he enjoyed cooking, his mother suggested selling home produce on a market stall and each weekend he would sell homemade cakes, biscuits, meringues, jams etc, which proved to be such a great success that Galton knew he had found his niche.

He went on to work with John Tovey at Miller Howe in the Lake District where, because he had never been to catering college, he essentially did his training. Here he worked his way to Head Chef and it was in the Lake District that he met his wife. Galton stayed at Miller Howe for 10 years, but also worked for a time at Le Pierre in New York and The Mount Nelson in Cape Town, South Africa.

Born and bred in Norfolk, he had always wanted to return and after some searching, found and bought Morston Hall in 1992 where he remains to this day. He achieved a Michelin star in 1999 and has 3 rosettes. He is also a fellow of the Craft Guild of Chefs.

Whilst Morston Hall continues to develop and evolve, Galton has recently entered the fast food industry, investing in Number 1 at Cromer, a fish and chip restaurant and takeaway. This year, so far has been a phenomenal success and proved to be an interesting learning curve.

CHEF'S VIEW

"I have known Peter for many, many years and when he invited me to get involved with this project I was delighted. Whilst knowing that Peter has had personal experience with this disease, I also assume I was asked because of my approach to cooking and working with the ingredients. My cooking ethics are simplicity, seasonality and provenance of the ingredients and this creates simple, clean recipes which would be beneficial to anyone eating for a healthier lifestyle.

Also as an added bonus, Michel Roux Snr has added his endorsement to this book and as he is such a huge icon to me, I just had to be part of it."

Jason Atherton

In 1996 Jason was named Best Young Chef in Britain by Jonathan Meades of the Sunday Times. He followed this in 1998 to become the first British chef to complete a stage at Spain's famous elBulli restaurant and this experience laid the foundations for his unique creative style.

Jason has worked under Pierre Koffmann, Nico Ladenis and Marco Pierre White as well as working for the Gordon Ramsay Group as executive chef for Verre in Dubai.

In 2005 he returned to the UK and opened maze in the heart of London and in 2007, with Gordon Ramsay, he oversaw the launch of maze in the Hilton Prague Old Town.

He left Gordon Ramsay holdings in 2010 to launch his own restaurant company and his flagship restaurant, Pollen Street Social opened in April 2011. Within 6 months, it was awarded a Michelin star and today holds 3 AA rosettes.

In 2011 he opened the tapas bar Esquine in Chinatown, Singapore and went on to open Pollen in June 2012, situated in Singapore's new downtown.

In March 2013 he opened his second Mayfair restaurant Little Social, to critical acclaim and then opened his third London restaurant, Social Eating House, in Poland Street, Soho.

Jason is an active patron to the David Nichols Spinal Injury Foundation, Hospitality Action, and regularly volunteers with other charities including Leuka 2000, where his efforts have raised over £2m.

CHEF'S VIEW

"When Peter Marshall contacted me about this book, I was honoured to be asked to contribute to such an amazing project. I am passionate about healthy eating for many reasons, eating well is essential for living a longer and more energetic life and I have two young and active daughters, who keep me on my toes!

Peter told me that he wanted to help those who had gone through similar experiences to his, and to make their healing process as comfortable as possible through maintaining a healthy diet, and embracing their love of food.

The recipes I have included are all nutrient-rich and high in protein – fish, lean meat, vegetables, fruit, eggs and dairy products are all on the menu. These recipes are easy to follow, balanced and include some great flavour combinations. After a long battle, survivors like Peter should enjoy cooking – and eating – healthy, nutritious and most importantly, delicious meals."

John Williams

British born John Williams brought some three decades of hospitality experience to The Ritz London when he joined the venerated kitchens of the legendary Piccadilly hotel as Executive Chef in 2004.

The son of a Tyneside fisherman, John developed his passion for food at an early age. that passion endures, as does his culinary philosophy: use ingredients of the highest quality, use them at their seasonal best and marry best of British dishes with Escoffier influenced classical French recipes to achieve distinctive, sublime creations.

After studying or his City and Guilds at South Shields College and at Westminster College, he began his culinary career at the Royal Garden Hotel in Kensington, followed by the position of Chef Director at Le Crocodile Restaurant. In 1986 he joined the distinguished Savoy Group of Hotels achieving an impressive 18 year tenure at both The Berkeley and Claridge's.

A member of the Academy of Culinary Arts for the past 20 years, Williams was appointed Executive Chairman in 2004 where he continues to work tirelessly to promote the education and training of young chefs. The recipient of numerous awards throughout his career, John is the proud holder of a Chevalier de l'Ordre du Mérite Agricole and a disciple Le Consiel Magistral de Disciples d'Auguste Escoffier. Furthermore, in 2008 he received the most distinguished award of his career with an MBE in the New Year's Honours List for his services to hospitality.

CHEF'S VIEW

"When Michel Roux initially put Peter Marshall and I in touch with regards to the cookery book, I was only too happy to participate in such a worthy and important cause, knowing how it has affected friends and family throughout my life. Health and happiness are such important things, and if I can provide a little, (or a lot!) of each of these with the food I produce then I feel I have done something towards the wellbeing of others.

The importance of being able to dine with food that stimulates the palate and brings enjoyment is the reason for me being in this profession for so many years; with the knowledge that this cookery book gives those who are in recuperation a little more of such pleasures in life, then I am only too happy to provide recipes that are simple on the palate and easy to make."

Mark Jordan

At the age of 15, Mark started working for Keith Floyd where he remained for 3 years.

From there, he went to the Gordleton Mill Hotel and Restaurant as sous chef to Jean-Christophe Novelli, which gained a Michelin star and 5 rosettes within a couple of years.

He became head pastry chef at Llangoed Hall for Bernard Ashley and then head pastry chef for the Roux brothers at the Grand Hotel in Amsterdam.

Coming back to England, he went to Rascasse in Leeds where he earned a Michelin star.

He was then invited to head up the team at the acclaimed Pink Geranium in Cambridge where he stayed for 9 years, leaving to go to Gilpin Lodge in the Lake District as Head Chef where he earned 3 rosettes. It was from here he was head hunted to the Atlantic Hotel on Jersey, where he has since gained 1 Michelin star and 4 rosettes.

Mark has just opened Mark Jordan at the Beach, which features relaxed Michelin standard food and has already earned a Michelin bib gourmand.

"I have known and been friends with Peter for a number of years ever since I participated in Cooking with Balls, a cookery book published for Ben Kay's testimonial and this involvement resulted in Peter publishing my own cookery book, Ocean Voyage.

When Peter approached me about participating in this book I jumped at the opportunity. My sister-in-law is currently in remission from the disease and my mother had leukaemia and as well as knowing Peter's history with cancer, I felt that this was a subject very close to my heart.

I have created these recipes specifically for this book bearing in mind the ingredients guidance we all received from Kelly at the LOC. This has definitely been an interesting learning curve for me and I also feel that this book will contain healthier eating options for everybody. My wife and I will definitely be using it as future reference to a healthier eating lifestyle for ourselves."

Peter Fiori

Peter Fiori has been the Executive Chef at Coutts, the Private Bank and Wealth Manager for over ten years.

His love affair with healthy food started at a very young age in Italy at the family home, nestled in the tiny mountain village of Cerretoli in Garfagnana, Tuscany. Looking back he believes that it was probably destiny to become a chef after remembering so clearly the sheer enjoyment of tasting that first home grown tomato, simply sliced with olive oil, rock salt and freshly ground black pepper – he was probably no more than four years old.

It was this early introduction to the finest and freshest vegetables and fruit that installed into his DNA, a passion for locally sourced produce and throughout his career he has made it his goal to constantly use seasonal products.

CHEF'S VIEW

"To me, fresh food is the key to a successful dish and I cannot emphasise enough how important it is for its increased nutritional value, as well as flavour intensity, smell and vibrancy.

In 2012, I was fortunate enough to be able to bring another dream to reality when we launched a fully functional vegetable garden to the roof terrace of the Coutts' HQ on the Strand in central London. Within months, we had 14,000 plants and trees growing, including berries, vegetables, all manner of herbs and edible flowers. Today, every dish that we produce in our kitchen contains some element from the garden and I aim to serve all dishes within two hours of harvest.

The garden has bought with it many unforeseen additional benefits, for example the enthusiasm of my young chefs as they grow and pick produce still gives me a buzz, and 18 months on we continue to have new ideas each day for what could be planted, grown or created. It was also the publicity around the garden that led me to be invited to provide recipes for the book.

Today, I'm honoured to be a contributor to 'Recipes for Life' and dedicate it to my dearest sister, Livia, whose life was tragically cut short by leukaemia in 1997."

Sam Moody

Sam Moody

Sam Moody is the Head Chef of the one and only Michelin-starred restaurant in the very beautiful city of Bath. A protégé of Michael Caines MBE, Sam has worked exclusively for the Andrew Brownsword Hotels 'Gidleigh Collection' since June 2005. Sam joined as a commis chef at the two-Michelin starred Gidleigh Park Hotel in Chagford, Devon and progressed to become chef tournand. Sam has worked at The Bath Priory March 2009, starting as sous chef and then head chef six months later. In September 2012 The Bath Priory restaurant was awarded a Michelin star and Sam was promoted to his present role.

Sam is actively involved with the City of Bath College and is a member of two fund-raising chefs' forums: The South West Chefs' and The Cotswolds Chefs'. He has twice represented Bath in the City-Twinning Association, with culinary demonstrations in Aix-en-Provence in 2011 and 2012.

Originally from Horley in Surrey, Sam moved to Cuckfield in West Sussex to work for Head Chef Steve Crane and left his Michelin-starred Ockenden Manor three years later to join Michael Caines.

CHEF'S VIEW

"When Peter approached Nick Halliday, our Chief Executive to ask if I would like to get involved in this book, I quickly realised how challenging it is to create and cook really tasty meals without using salt as well as staying within the ingredient guidelines available to use. I soon came to realise that for someone who really enjoys food and its flavours, this must be an added difficulty to a difficult time. So, as I sat down thinking about the recipes, I found that I was getting more and more involved with the thought process and started taking it much more seriously.

The recipes I have given to this book have been created specifically, although some of them are a variation of dishes I cook at Bath Priory, but I will definitely be using what I have learnt from this experience in the future within my cooking at the Bath Priory, as well as at home."

Simon Boyle

Simon Boyle is the vision behind Brigade and Beyond Food Foundation. Having started as an apprentice chef aged 16 at The Savoy, Simon has lead a highly respectable career since, working for Anton Mosiman, Saudi Princes, taking Head Chef roles on 5* Cruise Ships, becoming the first ever Culinary Ambassador for the global giant Unilever and running his own Private Catering and Events business.

Since 2004, Simon has worked tirelessly to help homeless people across London to rebuild their lives, using food as a catalyst, imparting his passion, skills and knowledge of cooking and food on to them and encouraging them to move their lives forward.

Brigade was born out of Simon's realisation that there are not enough inspirational projects aimed at supporting homeless people to end the cycle of 'no job no home – no home no job'. Simon Boyle's charity, Beyond Food Foundation runs two programmes which have been designed, implemented and perfected by Simon; Freshlife and United Kitchen.

Today, Brigade is expertly managed by De Vere Venues, but it is Simon's philosophy that is at the heart of it, and whether it is the venue for a business meeting, family gathering, or team building Cook School, Brigade will add a new level to your experience.

CHEF'S VIEW

"I had an extra ordinary relationship with my wife Annette. Not only did we share our family life together, enjoying our children Hope and Joseph, we had great holidays, long walks with our dog Bernie and a host of hobbies.

For many years, we worked together developing our own private dining and events company Beyond Food, eventually opening a joint venture social enterprise restaurant Brigade on Tooley Street in London and our own charity the Beyond Food Foundation.

In October 2011 Annette was diagnosed with lung cancer, unfortunately by the time we found out it had already spread. We couldn't believe it and decided to fight with aggressive treatment and a positive attitude.

Her treatment regime was cruel to say the least, but her spirit was incredible. One thing that helped was her diet. Trying to eat well is always good when you are ill and when she could, she would want me to cook food that would have a positive effect on her body. I would read up and research ingredients that would either fight cancer cells or help her feel a little better. I would also indulge her, when she'd let me.

We lost my darling girl on the 6th April 2013; cancer is a devastating disease that needs to be fought on so many levels. None more so than research to try and bring it to an end. That's why I really wanted to get involved with this project. I hope it raises money and that my recipes that I cooked for her can help others.

We miss her so much."

Steve Drake

Steve Drake's career has taken him from Southend Technical College to running his own, Michelin-starred, restaurant in Ripley, Surrey. His path includes stints in The Ritz Hotel, then working with Marco-Pierre White and latterly the legendary Nico Ladenis at Chez Nico in Park Lane. Steve still cites Nico as one of the chefs who has given him the greatest inspiration. A 'stage' with Marc Veyrat in the kitchens of his three Michelin-starred restaurant in Lake Annecy was his main prize for becoming a Roux Scholar back in 2001 and subsequently he has enjoyed educational trips to Italy, Dubai, and most recently Japan with the other scholars.

All these early influences have added rigour to his culinary armoury and since opening Drake's with his wife Serina in 2004, his repertoire has developed - as has his self-assurance. Steve says that "his inspiration has been my personal flavour discovery – hence the names of our two tasting menus, Flavour Journey and Flavour Discovery. We are confident in our own style of food, which is British but with a lightness and individuality which is just our own!"

Drake's is now moving steadily up the list of the top 100 restaurants in the country.

CHEF'S VIEW

"I have always been a strong advocate of the benefits of healthy eating and its importance in our daily lifestyle. Sadly, cancer seems to have touched most families today, including my own: Some years ago I lost my father to the disease, and at that time there was neither the knowledge, nor the emphasis, placed on the role a healthy diet can contribute. He wouldn't have even known that changes in his diet might have helped him.

It is a sad fact that with all today's technology and educational tools at our fingertips, so many people just aren't aware that a few simple modifications to their diet can help them fight this awful disease and play a key role in their recovery. Anything that can be done to promote the message of healthy eating is good, but particularly when it can help people at such a difficult time.

I am proud and pleased to have been invited to take part in this important project. This book is a great educational tool, and as chefs we can play a key part in helping make these healthy ingredients more exciting, interesting and creative. I have tried to make my recipes quick and simple in order to encourage readers to experiment – I wish you and your loved ones good health!"

Introduction

By Kelly McCabe

I f you are reading this book you, or someone you love, is likely to have been affected by cancer. There are currently 2 million people in the UK living with or after cancer treatment, and a further 14 million cancer survivors in the United States. This number is set to grow year on year as our ability to cure cancer and our life expectancy increases. Cancer is undoubtedly a life-changing experience and the period after cancer treatment is often used as a springboard to make healthy lifestyle choices including dietary changes.

With that in mind, this cook book has been developed through a collaboration of experts in the field of oncology and leading chefs to inspire people to try new things and to be confident when deciding what dietary changes they should make. It is not intended to be a scientific text book that explains nutrition research in detail but is instead filled with simple delicious recipes, practical advice and beautiful photography.

Use this book as you please; dip in and out of it when you need a little inspiration or create your own weekly meal plans. After reading this book and trying out some of the recipes it is hoped that you will feel confident enough to develop your own recipes, try some different cooking techniques and sample new ingredients. The recipes and information contained within this book present the most up-to-date guidance regarding eating well after cancer in the most practical way possible.

SEIZING THE WINDOW OF OPPORTUNITY

It is well known that changes to our lifestyle such as stopping smoking, reducing our alcohol intake, exercising more and eating a better diet can reduce our risk of certain types of cancer and of other illnesses such as heart disease or diabetes. However, it is equally well known that making long-term lifestyle changes can be challenging and frustrating and often requires a great deal of motivation and support. Many people find that after a cancer diagnosis they are more receptive to the idea of making lifestyle changes and will actively seek advice regarding diet and exercise. This moment of realisation and determination is sometimes termed a 'window of opportunity'. This book is designed to help you seize that window of opportunity and make beneficial dietary changes that will not only improve your health but also recover your enjoyment of eating, something that is often lost during cancer treatment. It is hoped that the pure enjoyment of good food will enable you to sustain this new healthy eating pattern lifelong. ▶

Leaders in Oncology Care

WHY IS NUTRITION IMPORTANT AFTER A CANCER DIAGNOSIS?

Deciding what to eat after a cancer diagnosis can be a highly emotive and confusing subject. In such a difficult time food can become the one thing that people feel they retain complete control over. Eating well during and after your treatment can help you to tolerate the treatment, accelerate your recovery afterwards, reduce your risk of the cancer returning and improve your general health and well-being.

Most scientists would agree that nutrition can be a confusing field but the good news for anyone hoping to find the best diet for them is that the advice given for cancer prevention is the same as that given to cancer survivors and mirrors the recommendations to reduce the risk of other diseases such as heart disease and diabetes. There is no need for different members of the same household to eat different diets instead the same healthy balanced approach is suitable for all.

Nutritional science is a dynamic, growing field and new research is published on a daily basis. Yet, although our understanding grows day by day, the fundamentals of good nutrition have remained the same for many years.

This book is designed to help affirm the basic principles of healthy eating whilst highlighting meal patterns and particular ingredients which may have a special role to play in the management and prevention of cancer. We are not going to delve into the science too much as this is well documented elsewhere.

UNDERSTANDING NUTRITION RESEARCH:

I often hear people remark on how frustrating and confusing nutrition research can be; what's good for us one day can be harmful the next. Over the last few years multiple different foods have been promoted as super-foods, from the exotic sun-dried shitake through to the humble chicken egg. Certainly in the years following the publication of this book nutrition researchers will go on to discover the beneficial properties of chemicals in many more of our staple plant foods. Many of the ingredients included in this book have been chosen because there is some evidence to suggest that they may possess beneficial properties for people following a cancer diagnosis.

IT IS ALWAYS PREFERABLE TO TRY TO MEET YOUR NUTRITIONAL REQUIREMENTS THROUGH FOOD RATHER THAN RELYING ON NUTRITIONAL SUPPLEMENTS:

Supplements should be used with caution, as some contain mega-doses of nutrients which can have a detrimental rather than helpful effect, particularly during cancer treatment.

The most prudent diet you can follow is one that is made up of predominately plant based foods e.g. fruits, vegetables, herbs, spices, beans or lentils, nuts, seeds and whole-grains such as rice and oats. Supplement this with plenty of fresh fish, eggs and a small amount of poultry whilst minimising your intake of processed and red meats, refined sugar and salt and you are well on your way to a nutrition-packed healthy diet that will help to lower your risk of disease.

Crash course in Cancer nutrition:

If you have completed treatment for cancer and want to know what to eat now or if you want to reduce your risk of cancer and improve your overall health the simple rules below would set you on the right path. These guidelines have been adapted from the recommendations of the World Cancer Research Fund. All of the recipes in this book have been carefully designed to meet these guidelines.

1. If you are overweight try to reach a healthy body mass index (BMI) and reduce your calorie intake to avoid weight gain. Maximise the nutritional value of your food whilst minimising calories by avoiding empty calories that offer no benefit such as those derived from refined sugar and saturated fat. If you are underweight, or would like to recover weight lost during treatment, do this by increasing your intake of nutrient-dense high energy foods such as nuts, avocado, olive oil, dark chocolate, Greek yoghurt and milky puddings.

2. Increase your intake of fruits, vegetables, legumes, nuts, seed and wholegrains. Try to include at least two portions of fruits or vegetables in every meal and at least one portion of pulses per day e.g. add a handful of lentils to your soup or salad at lunch, or serve some beans with your evening meal. If you are experiencing changes in bowel habits since your cancer treatment, you may need to modify the fibre content of your diet, for example, by choosing peeled and cooked fruits and vegetables instead of raw, or using nut butters instead of whole nuts and seeds. It is worth seeking specialist advice as some of the recipes in this book may need to be adapted to suit your specific needs.

3. Try to limit your red meat intake to once per week and limit salted or smoked meats to no more than once per fortnight. This includes bacon, ham and chorizo. Instead use fish, poultry, pulses, nuts, eggs or low-fat yoghurt as healthy high-protein alternatives.

4. Have omega-3 rich oily fish such as salmon, trout, sardines, mackerel, herring and fresh tuna two-three times per week.

5. Keep your blood glucose level stable and energy levels high by limiting refined carbohydrates including sugary breakfast cereals, white bread, white pasta, cakes, biscuits or sweets. Instead go for slow-release carbohydrates such as oats, wholegrain pasta, wild rice, quinoa or sweet potato. Try to include a small, handful-sized portion with every meal.

6. If overweight, or of a healthy body weight, limit the total amount of fat in your diet by choosing low-fat dairy products, reducing the amount of oil you add during cooking and avoiding fried foods. Instead include smaller amounts of healthy fats found in rapeseed oil, olive oil, nuts and avocado. Only if you are trying to regain weight after treatment should you use full fat varieties of such products.

7. Learn to flavour your food with pepper, herbs, spices and citrus juice rather than relying on salt. Remove the salt shaker from your kitchen if possible.

8. Minimise your alcohol intake and aim to have at least two consecutive alcohol-free days per week.

By making small, gradual changes to your diet you can stick to these rules whilst still enjoying your food! Follow the 80:20 rule; as long as you eat this way most of the time, the occasional treat is perfectly fine - whether that be a good quality glass of red wine, a fillet steak or a chocolate pudding. No food should be forbidden and it is for this reason that we have included some 'indulgent treats' throughout the book.

The Indulgent Treat Symbol

This symbol is used to indicate dishes which have a higher fat or sugar content, they are useful for people who may need to regain some weight after treatment and could also be used as a comforting treat for those times when we all need a lift. The 'indulgent' recipes still include plenty of nutrient packed ingredients to make sure they are not just providing 'empty calories'.

At-a-glance guide to using ingredients

	BE GENEROUS WITH...	USE IN MODERATION...	THINK OF ALTERNATIVES FOR...	NOTES
DAIRY	(Semi) skimmed milk Natural yoghurt Eggs Soya cream Oat/almond/ hazelnut/rice milk	Any good quality cheese Crème Fraiche	Full fat milk Cream Soya milk	Use full fat variations of dairy produce sparingly; opting for skimmed varieties instead helps to reduce the amount of saturated fat in your diet. Similarly, use small amounts of good quality cheese to add flavour to dishes, rather than using cheese as main ingredient. Use eggs as a healthy alternative to meat as they are a great source of protein, iron and vitamin D.
MEAT	Chicken Turkey Rabbit	Beef Lamb Mutton Pork Veal Venison Liver Duck Goose Game birds	Processed (cured or smoked) meat	Limit your red meat intake to once per week. If using poultry try to reduce the amount and add in some plant based protein sources e.g. lentils or beans to complete the dish. Processed (cured or smoked) meat e.g. ham, bacon, chorizo or salami should be avoided. Cooking meats at lower temperatures for a longer period of time e.g. casseroling, reduces the formation of potentially cancer-causing compounds produced when meat is fried or grilled at higher temperatures. Removing the skin and fat from cuts of meat before cooking helps to reduce the saturated fat content.
FISH	**Oily Fish:** Anchovies, Eel, Herring, Kipper, Mackerel, Pilchards, Wild Salmon, Sardines, Trout, Tuna steak **White Fish:** Cod, Coley, Haddock, Halibut, Plaice, Red Snapper, Sea Bass, Sole, Skate, Sea Bream, Tilapia, Turbot	Smoked fish. Larger fish e.g. shark or swordfish (use sparingly due to contaminant issues).		Think of ways to cook the fish without adding extra fat through frying i.e. baking/steaming. Fish should be featured plentifully in a cancer protective diet with a particular focus on omega-3 rich oily fish.

	BE GENEROUS WITH...	USE IN MODERATION...	THINK OF ALTERNATIVES FOR...	NOTES
PLANT PROTEINS	Seeds e.g. Pumpkin, Sesame, Sunflower, Chia and Flax Edamame (Soy) beans, Tempeh or Tofu Lentils or beans – all varieties	Nuts (all varieties) e.g. Brazil, Cashew, Pecan, Walnut, Pistachio	Peanuts	As a general rule, all of us should be moving towards a pattern of eating fish at least 3 times per week, lowering our meat intake and having at least two meat-free days per week. We can do this by using a variety of plant based protein sources instead e.g. lentils, chickpeas, beans (all varieties), nuts and seed, soya beans, tofu and tempeh.
FRUITS AND VEGETABLES	As many as possible – trying to get at least two into each meal time	Dried fruits Vegetable juices / smoothies	Fruit juices / smoothies	Cooking vegetables for shorter periods helps to retain important water soluble vitamins; steaming or stir-frying are good options. It is preferable to eat whole fruits as opposed to fruit juices or smoothies which can have a particularly high fructose content. See the smoothie/ juice section of this book for some healthier vegetable-based smoothie recipes.
STARCHES/ GRAINS/ FLOURS	Quinoa Basmati, Wild, Red Camargue rice Whole wheat pasta/ Spelt Wholegrain/ seeded breads Butternut Squash Pumpkin Sweet potato	White pasta White potato	White bread White flour (and things made from this e.g. cakes, biscuits and pastry).	Choose whole grains as opposed to refined carbohydrate foods wherever possible. Serving starches and grains with some protein or fat helps to slow the release of the sugars and stabilise blood glucose levels. Think about the balance of carbohydrate, and protein within each meal.
HERBS & SPICES	All except salt		Salt	Most herbs and spices contain important phytochemicals that can offer health benefits. Use plentifully in cooking to add both flavour and nutrition.
FATS / OILS	Olive oil Rapeseed oil Nut oils Avocado oil	Sunflower oil Corn oil Sesame oil	Butter Coconut oil Palm oil Margarine	Use oil sparingly in cooking – the aim is to limit total fat intake. Saturated fats, e.g. butter or coconut oil, can be used sparingly when cooking at high heat e.g. sautéing or frying as they are more stable. Olive oil or nut oils should be added after cooking, or used as salad dressings, for flavour as they are less able to withstand high temperatures.

The ingredient selection process:

The aim was for each chef to provide 10 recipes which fall in line with healthy eating guidelines outlined in the nutrition crash course and include plenty of the beneficial ingredients listed below.

When looking at the ingredients listed below it is important to emphasise that there is no such thing as a 'super food'! No one food in isolation can have a profound effect on our health or provide all the nutrients we need. Instead we should strive for a 'super-diet' which includes a wide range of these so-called super-foods, a thought-through dietary regimen that provides all of the nutrients we need without requiring excessive supplementation.

HERBS & SPICES

TURMERIC

A mild, fragrant spice from the ginger family. The active ingredient in turmeric is **curcumin** which has been found to have anti-inflammatory properties and is a powerful antioxidant.

CHILLI PEPPER

Chilli or cayenne peppers contain **capsaicin**, a plant chemical found to reduce pain when applied topically, plus vitamin A and carotenoids the pigments that give red, yellow, and orange plants their colour and have antioxidant properties.

GINGER

Ginger has been used as an anti-sickness remedy for hundreds of years as it contains volatile oils such as **gingerol**. These volatile oils are believed to stimulate saliva and gastric function.

FRUITS & VEG

RED GRAPES

The skin of red grapes contains **resveratrol**, a compound shown to reduce inflammation and have antioxidant properties. Both laboratory and animal studies have investigated the anti-cancer effects of resveratrol but human studies are lacking.

AVOCADO

Avocado is rich in heart-healthy **mono-unsaturated fatty acids**, such as oleic acid (the type found in olive oil) and the antioxidant vitamins C and E.

TOMATOES

Tomatoes contain **lycopene** an antioxidant chemical found to confer protection against prostate cancer. Lycopene gives tomatoes their red pigment and is more readily absorbed from processed tomato products such as tomato purée or cooked tomatoes than raw tomatoes.

CRUCIFEROUS VEG E.G. BROCCOLI, KALE, KOHLRABI, CABBAGE, CAULIFLOWER, BOK CHOI, CRESS, ROCKET

The cruciferous vegetable family are packed with **sulphurofanes**. Several studies have linked an increased intake of these sulphur compounds to a lower cancer risk, particularly for prostate cancer.

ALLIUM VEG E.G. GARLIC, ONION, SHALLOT, CHIVES, LEEKS

Onions and garlic contain sulphur compounds found to help lower blood pressure. Some studies have found that garlic helps to strengthen the immune system during cancer treatment. Onions also have a high concentration of **quercetin** which has anti-inflammatory benefits. Garlic contains a unique sulphur compound, **allicin**, which promotes antioxidant activity and has powerful antibacterial and antiviral functions.

OTHER

OILY FISH

Contain **Omega-3** fatty acids found to help ameliorate our natural inflammatory response.

EGGS

Eggs are a naturally rich source of iron, vitamin D and a rich mixture of **amino acids**, the building blocks of proteins. The easily digestible protein in eggs helps to suppress our appetite and can aid weight loss efforts.

BRAZIL NUTS

Brazil nuts are one of very few dietary sources of **selenium**, a mineral integral to our immune function. Try to have 1-2 every day.

DARK CHOCOLATE (COCOA)

The cocoa bean is packed full of protective **flavonols** which have antioxidant qualities and have been shown to improve vascular health. Buy chocolate with the highest cocoa content (more than 70%) for maximum effect.

SOY

A higher intake of soy products, containing the **isoflavones genistein** and **daidzein**, has been linked with a reduced risk of certain cancers and lower cholesterol levels.

GREEN TEA

Polyphenol and antioxidant rich green tea has been advocated as having anti-cancer properties for hundreds of years. The active constituent is **epigallocatechin-3-gallate** (EGCG), which accounts for 40% of the total polyphenol content of green tea extract. Aim to have 2-3 cups per day.

CONTENTS

LIVING WELL AT LOC

A programme of care during treatment and beyond...

Dr Michelle Kohn

LOC believes that it is vital to care for every element of the cancer patient's wellbeing. This is why it offers the Living Well programme. Living Well is a selection of workshops, lectures and clinics to help support patients through their treatment and to improve their lifestyle once their treatment is complete. It also offers family members a parallel programme of care.

It covers all kinds of issues from providing medical information about treatment side-effects such as fatigue, to helping patients cope with psychological problems such as depression and anxiety. It also helps people to rebuild their lives after treatment finishes, offering expert advice on how to cope with ongoing side-effects, as well as practical ways to make healthy lifestyle changes.

Programme director Dr Michelle Kohn, Specialist in Supportive Cancer Care, formerly Medical Advisor to Macmillan Cancer Support and Breakthrough Breast Cancer, founded the programme back in 2009 and is passionate about Living Well.

'This is a programme that we offer without charge, to patients with any type of cancer and at any stage of treatment (or beyond), who are referred to us by LOC oncologists and other specialists,' she explains.

'We aim to minimise the worry, confusion and stress of cancer treatment and its aftermath, working closely with LOC oncologists. Our multi-disciplinary team of cancer experts offers lectures, group workshops or one-to-one consultations. We give patients access to reliable, up-to-date information, as well as individualised support.

'We are there for all our patients, whatever their age, type of cancer or stage of treatment. We are also there to support family members. Much of our guidance focusses on general good health, for instance, we have workshops on diet or exercise because simple lifestyle changes can enable recovery. But we can also tailor what we offer to meet specific needs and situations. For instance, one person might want to know more, from an expert, about the genetic aspects of their cancer whilst another may have very specific medical side-effects to cope with.

Group workshops offer a mutually supportive environment. 'You see some people hesitantly arrive thinking 'what am I doing here?' but it can be immensely helpful to be with a group of people who have been through similar experiences, and who understand what you are going through. There is a tremendous sense of camaraderie and support.'

People often feel as if they are going into free fall after treatment. Anxiety, depression or practical worries are very common as you piece your life back together. Living Well aims to make that transition easier too.

The multi-disciplinary team includes specialists in exercise, psychology, relaxation, sexual medicine and genetics, as well as nutrition, and a chef.

As Dr Kohn explains: 'Food is a major part of the Living Well programme not just because we love it, but because there is emerging evidence that good nutrition and weight management, combined with exercise, can make a real difference to how patients cope with cancer treatment and its side-effects, and may even have an impact on cancer recurrence. These skills really can improve quality of life and help to control symptoms. They can transform how a patient copes during treatment, and afterwards. We see nutrition as part of a 'holy trinity' of coping skills: learning to eat well, move well and think well.'

The Programme can help with common dilemmas such as 'should I take supplements?' or 'should I avoid certain foods?' However the aim is also to inspire participants to enjoy food again.

'In our group sessions, our dietitian Kelly McCabe offers invaluable nutritional information and answers patients' questions, whilst our chef Kevin Fine creates wonderful, fresh, simple food for everyone to share. He chats to patients, demonstrates techniques and gives practical tips for eating well. Kevin's mantra is: 'beware of packaging'; his top suggestion: 'only eat food that your great-grandma would recognise,' says Dr Kohn. He suggests wonderful ways to get flavour from herbs and spices, without using salt or saturated fats, and introduces delicious foods such as quinoa, that are new to many families.

All of the strategies – including the healthy eating plans - are designed to be very simple - so anyone can replicate them at home. The idea is to make lasting, healthy, ongoing changes.

'Perhaps above all our aim is to inspire patients to eat well,' says Dr Kohn. 'It is incredibly heartening to see this week after week: people who have stopped enjoying their food, taking pleasure again in eating well.

'This has a knock-on effect. When patients eat better and enjoy their food again, they feel better physically and emotionally: they become more active and engaged in other parts of their lives. One participant, a woman in her late forties who had been recently treated for breast cancer, felt so much better after changing her diet that she took up running again. She worked up to a 5km charity run and completed it in her fastest time ever. Another participant, a man in his late fifties who had finished treatment for bowel cancer, wrote that he felt better than ever after doing our six week course. 'The new normal,' he said, 'is better than the normal.'

'After our workshops, people often say, 'if only I'd known this from the start it would have been so much easier to cope... but my oncologist said just eat what you like'. So much distress could be avoided if cancer patients and their loved ones could have expert dietary advice immediately on diagnosis. Good nutrition should not take over your life, but it should certainly enhance it. Living Well is the human side of medicine, delivered in a personal way. I've seen eating well help hundreds of our patients, and I'm delighted that this cookbook will now bring it to so many more.'

With special thanks to Kevin Fine, Patricia Michelson and Lucy Atkins.

Recipes

Breakfast

PREPARATION TIME: 10 MINS

COOKING TIME: 25 MINS

Stewed prunes with cinnamon and orange

BY GALTON BLACKISTON

INGREDIENTS

450g Agen prunes

1 orange, cut into quarters

1 cinnamon stick

11g soft brown sugar

6 cloves

enough water to cover

INSTRUCTIONS

1. Place all the ingredients into a large saucepan and cover with cold water.
2. Slowly bring the pan to the boil, simmer for about 20-25 minutes until the prunes are soft.
3. Transfer to a large bowl, cool and store in the fridge.

Prunes are a great source of vitamin K and soluble fibre which can help to naturally regulate bowel habits and stabilise blood glucose levels.

This recipe is great served with low-fat natural yoghurt.

SERVES 2

PREPARATION TIME: 10-15 MINS

Vanilla scented natural yoghurt with honey, fresh red berries and oatmeal

BY MARK JORDAN

INGREDIENTS

250g natural yoghurt
1 vanilla pod
50g fresh raspberries
50g fresh strawberries
50g fresh cranberries
50g oatmeal
honey to taste

INSTRUCTIONS

1. In a bowl add the natural yoghurt and mix with a whisk.
2. Using a sharp knife, cut the vanilla pod lengthways and and using the back of the knife gently scrape out all the seeds. Add the seeds to the yoghurt and and mix well so all the vanilla seeds are evenly distributed through the yoghurt
3. Divide the yoghurt into two bowls, making sure to get all the bowls with the same amount in.
4. Sprinkle some of the raspberries, strawberries and the cranberries all over the top of the vanilla yoghurt. Follow this by sprinkling some of the oatmeal over the top.
5. Finally drizzle a little of the natural honey all over the top of the fruit and oatmeal. Serve straight away.

Adding good quality vanilla paste or fresh vanilla to yoghurt and fruit salads is a great way to sweeten the recipe without adding sugar.

SERVES
8-10

PREPARATION TIME: 20 MINS + PLUS
OVERNIGHT COOLING TIME

Bircher muesli

BY JOHN WILLIAMS

INGREDIENTS

muesli:
800g rolled oats
150g apricots, diced and dried
2 pears
6 apples
150ml honey
200ml orange juice
200ml apple juice
300ml low fat natural yoghurt
300ml reduced fat crème fraîche
1 tsp vanilla essence

topping:
80g strawberries
80g wild strawberries
80g raspberries
80g blueberries

INSTRUCTIONS

1. Place the rolled oats and the diced, dried apricots into a bowl.
2. Finely grate the pears and apples and combine with all the other ingredients.
3. Keep the mixture in the fridge overnight to allow the flavours to amalgamate, ensuring the mix is suitably loose.
4. Cut the larger strawberries into four and combine all of the fruits
5. Place the muesli into a glass and scatter 30-40g of fruit over the top to finish.

Unlike other breakfast cereals, whole rolled oats have no added salt and sugar. Soaking the oats overnight helps to break down their tough outer shell, releasing their nutrients and giving them a creamier consistency.

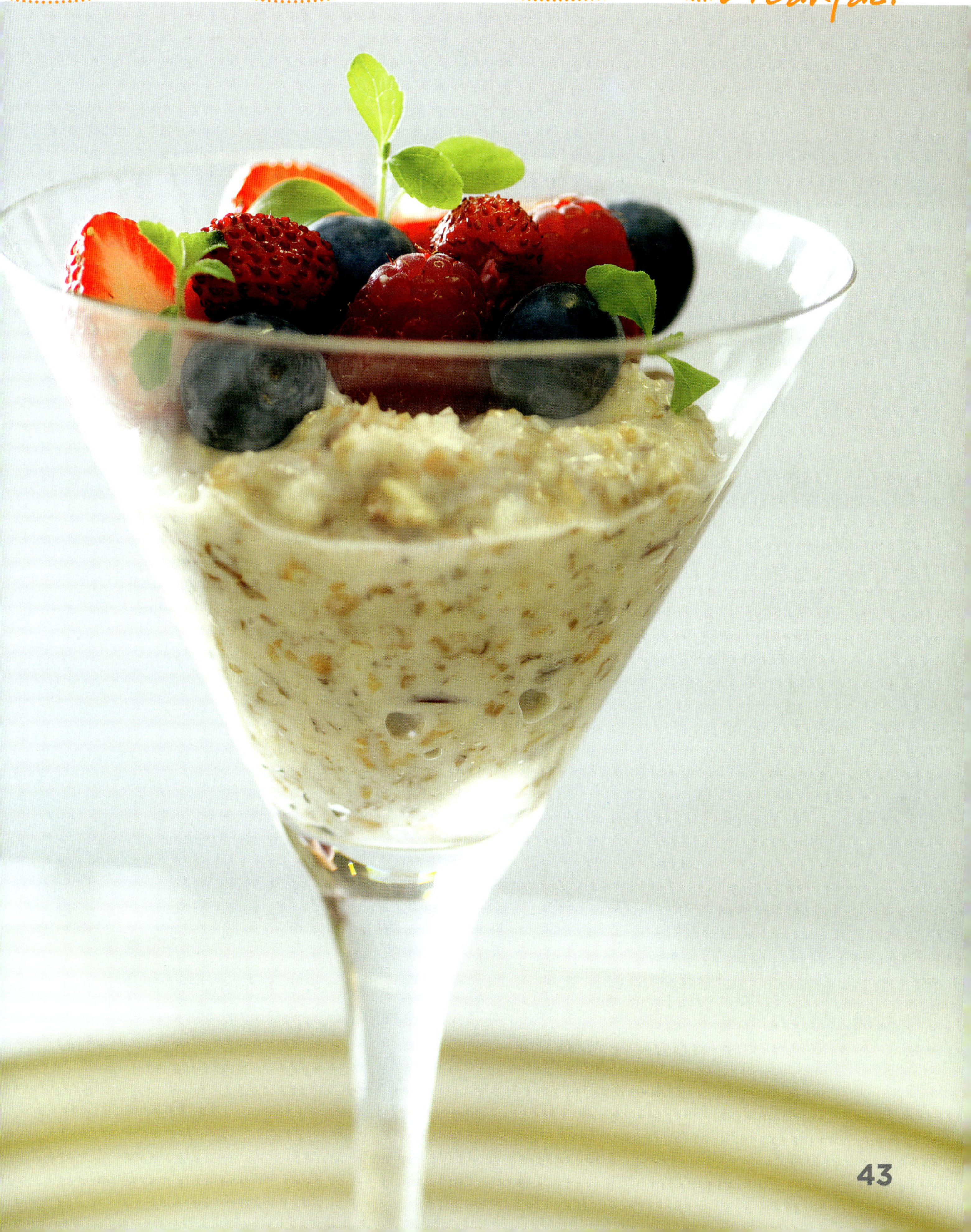

PREPARATION TIME: 5 MINS

COOKING TIME: 40 MINS

INGREDIENTS

granola:
60g whole unskinned almonds
40g brazil nuts
40g cashew nuts
350g rolled oats
50g pumpkin seeds
50g sunflower seeds
80g dried cranberries
100g dried apricots, roughly chopped

syrup:
3 tbs water
2 tbs rapeseed oil
2 tbs groundnut oil
240ml runny honey

other ingredients:
300ml low fat natural yoghurt
100g homemade granola
50g fresh blueberries

Home made granola, yoghurt and blueberries
BY ANDREW FAIRLIE

INSTRUCTIONS

1. Preheat the oven to 140°C. Roughly chop all the nuts put them into a large mixing bowl, add the oats and seeds and set aside.
2. Mix together the syrup ingredients, put into a small saucepan and heat gently. Pour the syrup over the nut mixture and mix well.
3. Line a large tray with baking parchment and spread the granola mix over evenly not any more than 1cm thick, if necessary use 2 trays.
4. Bake for 40 minutes, turning 2 or 3 times as it bakes, it should turn a golden honey colour. Remove from the oven.
5. While the granola is just warm stir in the fruits and leave on the tray to cool.
6. Pour the yoghurt into a bowl, sprinkle over the granola and top with the blueberries.

chef's tip:
This will keep for up to 12 weeks if stored in air-tight container.

Brazil nuts are an excellent source of selenium, a mineral that is integral to our immune function. Try to include 1-2 Brazil nuts every day.

SERVES 4

PREPARATION TIME: 30 MINS +
FREEZING TIME

Strawberry and hibiscus granita with honey and yoghurt

BY STEVE DRAKE

INGREDIENTS

500g strawberries

900ml water

50g dried hibiscus flowers (if you cannot purchase these then rose water can be used as a substitute)

1 tbsp honey

200ml low fat natural yoghurt

INSTRUCTIONS

1. Take 400g of strawberries, reserving 100g for the garnish, and add 400ml water. Bring to the boil and simmer for 5 minutes.

2. Remove from the heat and allow to drip through a cloth to obtain a clear liquid and chill.

3. Take 500ml of water and bring to the boil, add the dried hibiscus flowers and remove from the heat, allow to cool, chill and then strain to remove the flowers, leaving a hibiscus infusion.

4. Mix the honey and yoghurt together and chill.

5. Measure 450ml of the hibiscus infusion, adding 300ml of the strawberry juice to it and freeze in a shallow container.

6. Once frozen scrape with a fork to create the granita.

7. Chop the remaining strawberries and divide between 4 cocktail glasses, add a spoonful of the yoghurt and honey mix and finally fill the glass with the granita.

This is an extravagant but low-fat, nutritious breakfast that is perfect when entertaining guests. The granita can be made in advance and stored in the freezer – it also makes a healthy dessert.

PREPARATION TIME: 20 MINS

COOKING TIME: 5 MINS

Smoked salmon gateau with poached egg and lemon

BY SIMON BOYLE

INGREDIENTS

1 lemon, juiced and zested
250g fromage blanc
freshly ground black pepper,
    for seasoning
8 pancakes, pre-cooked
200g oak smoked salmon, sliced
1 tbsp white wine vinegar
4 fresh eggs
¼ bunch dill

INSTRUCTIONS

1. Dry the lemon zest in the airing cupboard, until it is granular like salt, this should take an hour or so.

2. In a bowl, season the fromage blanc with lemon juice and freshly ground pepper. Lay a pancake onto a plate and spoon 2 tablespoons of the fromage blanc and with the back of the spoon spread it around evenly. Lay a single layer of the smoked salmon from edge to edge, careful not to overlap it.

3. Repeat until you have layered all the salmon and used all the pancakes, leaving the final one with nothing on the top. Cover with cling film and place a similar sized weight on top (I suggest a pot with the same circumference with a bag of sugar). Press for an hour or until you need it.

4. When you're ready to serve, bring a small pan of water to the boil, add a splash of white wine vinegar, stir the water and crack in the eggs one by one. Poach until soft, take out and drain,

5. To serve, cut a wedge of the salmon gateau and place on a plate. Place an egg next to the gateau and season with the dried lemon zest and picked dill leaves.

Smoked salmon is a great source of both protein and omega-3 fats and therefore an ideal option for breakfast or brunch.

Wild mushrooms and herb omelette

BY DANIEL GALMICHE

SERVES 4

PREPARATION TIME: 20 MINS

COOKING TIME: 10 MINS

INGREDIENTS

200g girolles, or other
    wild mushrooms, trimmed
2 tbsp olive oil
few drops of squeezed lemon
1 bunch of parsley, chopped
1 clove of garlic, skin off, chopped
freshly ground black pepper, to taste
8 eggs

INSTRUCTIONS

1. Wash the girolles very carefully as they are fragile and break easily. Pat dry with a kitchen towel. If the girolles are large, just cut them in half, but they are better small and whole, Put the olive oil and a few drops of lemon into a bowl and marinate them for 30 minutes.

2. Put a non-stick pan over a medium heat, add a drizzle of olive oil. Drain and sauté the girolles for a few minutes or until they're a nice golden colour, then throw in the chopped parsley and garlic and season with pepper.

3. In a separate bowl, beat the eggs. Heat a non-stick pan on a medium heat and add a drizzle of olive oil. When the oil is warm, but not smoking, add the egg and cook until it still has a slightly runny consistency. Then place the girolle fricassee into the middle and by slightly lifting the pan, start to roll the egg omelette around the bottom of the pan. Then turn it out onto a serving plate to cut a portion for each of your guests.

Several studies have investigated the link between mushrooms and a reduced risk of cancer with encouraging results. Try using a variety of different mushrooms, each with their own unique nutritional properties and flavour e.g. girolle, chestnut, shiitake, reishi and oyster.

PREPARATION TIME: 15 MINS

COOKING TIME: 15 MINS

Baked beans, pata negra, poached egg

BY PETER FIORI

INGREDIENTS

baked beans:
1 small onion, chopped
2 tbsp olive oil
1 garlic clove, crushed
1 red chilli, chopped
2½ tsp cumin powder
2 tsp English mustard powder
2 tsp tomato purée
freshly ground black pepper
100ml low salt chicken stock
400g cooked haricot beans
juice ½ lemon

poached eggs:
dash malt vinegar
4 organic poached eggs

to serve:
16 slices pata negra
granary toast

INSTRUCTIONS

baked beans:
1. Fry the onion in the olive oil until slightly browned, add the garlic, chilli (including the seeds), cumin, mustard powder, tomato purée, pepper and gently cook for 5 minutes.
2. Add the chicken stock followed by the beans, gently stir and warm through. Remove from the heat and add a squeeze of lemon juice.

poached eggs:
1. Bring a deep pan of water to the boil and add a dash of malt vinegar. Gently simmer the water and drop in the eggs that have been decanted into a tea cup.
2. Cook gently for 4 minutes for a soft poached egg. Remove from the water and place on kitchen paper.

to serve:
Place the hot beans in the centre of the plate, top with the sliced pata negra ham, followed by the soft poached egg and drizzle with some olive oil. Serve with granary toast.

These baked beans are far tastier than the shop-bought alternative and offer a high protein, high fibre breakfast that will keep you fuelled until lunchtime.

This recipe is deemed 'indulgent' as it includes cured ham.
However, if served with just an egg it could be eaten more regularly.

AVOCADO

Fresh and tender

TOMATO

A good source of lycopene

PREPARATION TIME: 20 MINS

COOKING TIME: 3-3½ HRS

Perfect scrambled eggs with tomatoes on toast

BY JASON ATHERTON

INGREDIENTS

roasted tomatoes:
4 ripe plum tomatoes
1 garlic clove, peeled and
    thinly sliced
1 thyme sprig, leaves only
black pepper
olive oil, to drizzle

other ingredients:
6 eggs
75g butter
75ml milk
black pepper
4 thick slices granary bread, toasted

INSTRUCTIONS

1. Prepare the roasted tomatoes by preheating the oven to 100°C. Halve the tomatoes and arrange them, cut side up, on a baking tray. Scatter over the sliced garlic and thyme leaves. Sprinkle with a generous pinch of pepper and drizzle with olive oil. Roast for 3-3½ hours until the tomatoes are soft.

2. Now prepare the scrambled eggs by adding the eggs to a pan of simmering water and gently cooking for 7½-8 minutes. Drain and place under cold running water until cool enough to handle, then carefully peel off the shells.

3. The egg whites should be set but the yolks still runny. Cut the eggs in half and scoop out the runny yolks into a large bowl. Chop the egg whites very finely, then add to the egg yolks and mix well. (The eggs can be chilled if preparing ahead).

4. When ready to serve, put the chopped eggs in the pan with the butter, milk and seasoning. Stir over a medium-low heat until the egg yolks are scrambled but still creamy. Meanwhile toast the bread.

5. Place the hot toast slices in warm serving plates and drizzle over a little olive oil. Arrange the roasted tomato halves on the toast, pile with scrambled egg and serve.

This recipe takes a little extra time but is well worth the effort.
The roasted tomatoes can be prepared in advance and stored in an
air-tight jar in olive oil for a few days. Drain well before serving.
Cooking tomatoes in this way increases the availability of their
lycopene content.

Snacks

Guacamole on wholemeal bread
BY GALTON BLACKISTON

GUACAMOLE:

PREPARATION TIME: 15 MINS

INGREDIENTS

2 ripe avocados, skinned and chopped
juice of 2 limes
1 clove garlic, mashed
4 tbsp fresh coriander, chopped
1 red chilli, finely chopped
1 shallot, finely chopped
150ml olive oil
splash of Tabasco
freshly ground black pepper,
   for seasoning

INSTRUCTIONS

1. Place the chopped avocados into a bowl.
2. Pour over the lime juice followed by the rest of the ingredients.
3. Mix well, taste and season.
4. If you do not plan to use it straight away, to help prevent the guacamole from discolouring, put cling-film directly onto the guacamole to exclude the air. Set aside in a cool, dark place until needed.

OUR VERY POPULAR WHOLEMEAL BREAD:

MAKES 2 X 900G LOAVES

PREPARATION TIME: 10 MINS

COOKING TIME: 40 MINS

INGREDIENTS

700g wholemeal flour
225g strong plain flour, sifted
110g muesli, select a luxury fruity mix
10g sea salt
4 tbsp black treacle
725ml warm water
50g fresh baker's yeast

2 x 900G loaf tins lined with
greaseproof paper

INSTRUCTIONS

1. Place the 2 flours, muesli and salt in the bowl of a food mixer with the K beater or dough hook attachment.
2. In a measuring jug melt the treacle thoroughly with the warm water. Crumble the yeast on top of the liquid and leave to froth until it resembles the head of a pint of Guinness.
3. Turn the food mixer on to a low speed and slowly pour the liquid into the flour and muesli mixture so that it binds together. Leave the machine running for a further 5 minutes.
4. The end result should be a sloppy dough mix, which is just right for loaves of bread, but too wet to adapt to make bread rolls. Divide the dough mixture equally between the 2 lined loaf tins and pat down gently.
5. Place somewhere warm to prove for about 30 minutes, or until the dough has risen to the top of the tins.
6. Preheat the oven to 200°C and bake the loaves for 30-40 minutes. Remove from the oven and turn out onto a cooling rack.

60   RECIPES FOR LIFE

Avocados are a great source of heart-healthy monounsaturated fats plus Vitamin E, an antioxidant. Once you have mastered this quick and easy guacamole recipe it will become a lunchtime favourite.

PREPARATION TIME: 10 MINS

COOKING TIME: 20 MINS

Sweet potato and cumin compote

BY SAM MOODY

INGREDIENTS

1 sweet potato
½ tsp of cumin
20ml olive oil
freshly ground black pepper,
    for seasoning
50ml of water

INSTRUCTIONS

1. Peel and dice the sweet potato into a rough small dice.
2. Line a tray with tin foil, add the sweet potato and other ingredients, mix well and tightly cover with foil.
3. Cook at 160°C for 15-20 minutes or until the sweet potato is soft.
4. Once cooked mash the sweet potato with a fork.
5. Serve with coriander and some crackers.

Sweet potatoes are significantly more nutritious than their white counterparts. Their orange colour indicates that they are packed full of beta-carotene and vitamin C.

Grilled corn pimento mayonnaise

BY PETER FIORI

SERVES
4

PREPARATION TIME: 15 MINS

COOKING TIME: 75 MINS
(for the roast garlic)

INGREDIENTS

4 corn on the cobs
olive oil

roasted garlic:
1 bulb garlic
1 tbs olive oil
2 sprigs thyme

pimento mayonnaise:
low fat mayonnaise
1 tsp harissa
pinch paprika
juice ½ lemon
50g smoked piquillo peppers
pinch cayenne pepper
roasted garlic cloves

garnish:
basil shoots

INSTRUCTIONS

1. Place the corn in a pan of boiling water and cook for 5 minutes. Remove from the water and drain.
2. Rub the corn with olive oil and season.
3. Griddle until charred then cut each corn into 3 pieces.

roast garlic:
1. Place a bulb of garlic on silver foil, drizzle with olive oil and a few sprigs of thyme.
2. Enclose in the foil and roast at 160°C for 1 hour and 15 minutes until soft.
3. Cool and remove the garlic from its skin.

pimento mayonnaise:
1. In a blender, add the mayonnaise, harissa, paprika, lemon juice, smoked piquillo peppers, cayenne pepper and roasted garlic cloves.
2. Blend to create a pimento mayonnaise.

to serve:
Serve the corn with pimento mayonnaise and basil shoots.

Unlike most other vegetables, sweetcorn releases more phytochemicals the longer it is cooked for, therefore this recipe which boils and then chargrills the corn will ensure you obtain maximum nutritional value.

COOKING TIME: 10 MINS

Chilli and garlic peas

BY SAM MOODY

INGREDIENTS

25ml olive oil

1 large shallot

2 cloves garlic

1-2 red chillies (depending how hot you like it)

500g peas in the pod, or mange tout

INSTRUCTIONS

1. Heat a large frying pan or a wok and add the oil.
2. Slice the shallots, garlic and chilli, and sweat in the oil for 3 minutes.
3. Add the peas, fry for 2 minutes, add a splash of water to help the peas cook though. Cook for 3-5 minutes.
4. Serve.

This fibre-packed snack makes a great side-dish for fish or chicken too.

ASPARAGUS

Fresh and tender

GINGER

Adds warmth to soups and smoothies

PREPARATION TIME: 40 MINS

COOKING TIME: 40 MINS

Baba ghanoush

BY PETER FIORI

INGREDIENTS

2 aubergines
1 tbsp olive oil
100g yoghurt
juice ½ a lemon
3 grinds of fresh ground black pepper
2 cloves garlic

garnish:
50g walnuts
pomegranate seeds
coriander cress
optional: granary bread

INSTRUCTIONS

1. Prick the aubergines with a fork and cook over a gas flame for 10 minutes, turning all the time. The aubergines should be black and charred.

2. Place on a tray, cover with foil and roast in the oven at 150°C for 15 minutes.

3. Put in a plastic bag, leave to cool and then peel away all the skin and place in a colander with a weight on top and leave to drain.

4. Tip the aubergine flesh into a blender bowl, add the oil, yoghurt and lemon juice plus the 3 grinds of pepper.

5. Crush the garlic make a paste and add this to the bowl. Pulse in a blender to make a coarse paste. Place the baba ghanoush in a bowl ready to be garnished.

6. Roast the walnuts for 5 minutes, tip into a tea towel and rub to remove as much skin as possible. Place in a sieve to remove any dust then sprinkle on top of the baba ghanoush.

7. Top with pomegranate seeds, coriander cress and finish with a drizzle of yoghurt.

8. Serve with toasted granary bread.

This middle eastern inspired dish is great on its own or as part of a mezze. The pomegranate seed garnish is not essential but would add extra cancer-fighting crunch.

Vietnamese vegetable roll

BY JOHN WILLIAMS

SERVES
10

PREPARATION TIME: 30 MINS

INGREDIENTS

1 white radish
1 large shallot
2 carrots
2 celery sticks
1 fennel
5 spring onions
1½ tsp mayonnaise
½ lemon
20 leaves freshly cut coriander
10 leaves freshly cut mint
10 leaves freshly cut basil
1 red chilli
1 bunch chives
30g avocado mousse (purée of
   avocado, lemon, cream and
   seasoning)

INSTRUCTIONS

1. Cut a long sheet of pre-peeled white radish on a mandoline 2mm thick, trim to small rectangles of 7x4cm.
2. Cut all the other vegetables into very fine julienne, bind with a touch of mayonnaise, squeeze of lemon and finish with freshly cut herbs and finely chopped red chilli.
3. Place a small amount onto a rectangle of radish and roll to a perfect cylinder.
4. Trim and fasten with a chive and top each roll with avocado purée and caviar (optional).

The white radish, sometimes named Diakon or Mooli, is packed full of vitamin C and can be bought at any Asian grocers. However, if it is difficult to find, rice paper would make a suitable alternative.

SERVES
4

Cauliflower and hazelnut couscous

BY SAM MOODY

INGREDIENTS

300g cauliflower
50g hazelnuts
50ml olive oil
juice and zest 1 lemon
freshly ground black pepper,
   for seasoning

INSTRUCTIONS

1. Grate the cauliflower on a cheese grater, toast the hazelnuts, crush and add.
2. Mix in the rest of ingredients, allow to stand for 10 minutes.
3. Serve. Brilliant with fish or as a light snack.

This low-GI side-dish is a nutrient packed alternative to conventional cous-cous. Cauliflower, part of the cruciferous family, is packed full of protective phytochemicals, whilst the hazelnuts add extra protein and flavour.

This recipe takes a little extra time and effort but is an indulgent treat worth trying. Rabbit meat is considered "white" and therefore makes a great change from chicken or turkey.

Rabbit scrumpets, tarragon and mixed spice, roast beetroot

BY PETER FIORI

SERVES 4

PREPARATION TIME: MAKE SCRUMPET MIX THE DAY BEFORE, COOKING TIME 2-3 HRS

COOKING TIME: ON THE DAY, 15 MINS

INGREDIENTS

scrumpet mix:
2 rabbit legs
1 litre chicken stock
2 star anise
2 bay leaves
4 cloves
6 peppercorns, crushed
1 green chilli, deseeded and chopped
3 tbsp soy sauce

coating for scrumpets:
100g cornflour
2 beaten eggs
200g granary breadcrumbs
500ml ground nut oil

tarragon mayonnaise:
1 tbsp tarragon, chopped
6 tbsp low fat mayonnaise
1 tbsp Pernod
1 tsp lime juice

roast beetroot:
1 large beetroot
3 tbsp olive oil
2 sprig thyme
dash of olive oil

INSTRUCTIONS

scrumpet mix:
1. Place the rabbit legs in a small pot and barely cover with chicken stock.
2. Add the star anise, bay leaves, cloves, peppercorns and green chilli.
3. Bring to a gentle simmer, cover with a lid and cook in the oven at 150°C until the rabbit starts to fall off the bone (approximately 2-3 hours).
4. Flake the rabbit meat off the bone and shred it. Pass the remaining liquor and reduce to a thick syrup (50ml). Add to the rabbit, season with soy sauce and set in a tray with a weight on top. Place in the fridge.
5. When firm, cut into fingers and coat in the cornflour followed by the beaten eggs and finish with the granary bread.
6. Heat the ground nut oil to 160°C and drop in the rabbit scrumpets and fry until golden and hot in the centre.

tarragon mayonnaise:
Add the chopped tarragon to the mayonnaise with the Pernod and lime juice and blend.

roast beetroot:
Place the beetroots on silver foil, add a dash of olive and 2 sprigs of thyme and enclose in the foil. Roast in the oven at 180°C for approximately 1½ hours until tender.

to serve:
Slice the beetroots and serve with the scrumpets and mayonnaise.

Light
lunches

Pomegranate is a good source of fibre. It also contains vitamins A, C and E, iron and other antioxidants.

Seared mackerel with pomegranate and manuka honey dressing

SIMON BOYLE

SERVES
4

PREPARATION TIME: 50 MINS

COOKING TIME: 10 MINS

INGREDIENTS

dressing:

1 pomegranate

2 tsp Manuka honey

1 red pepper, fairly small dice

3 large fresh mint sprigs,
   finely chopped

3 tsp red wine vinegar

4 tbsp extra virgin olive oil

¼ tsp rose harissa (optional)

freshly ground black pepper,
   for seasoning

mackerel:

2 tbsp extra virgin olive oil

1 small spring green

½ red onion

1 lemon, zested and juiced

4 fresh mackerel fillets, pin boned and
   cut into two equal pieces

INSTRUCTIONS

dressing:

1. Cut the pomegranate into 4 quarters and de-seed. Collecting any escaping juice, place half the seeds in a food processor and blitz. Strain the juice and pour into a small pan, add the honey and bring to the boil, reduce by half.

2. Place all the other dressing ingredients into the bowl with the pomegranate juice and combine thoroughly, add the pomegranate seeds and reserve.

mackerel:

1. In a large shallow pan, heat some olive oil until very hot. Add the shredded spring green and stir-fry for 2-3 minutes. Add the sliced red onion and continue cooking for a further 2-3 minutes. Season with lemon rind, juice and pepper.

2. Heat a frying pan until quite hot and add the olive oil. Season the mackerel fillets and then place skin side down in the hot frying pan. Cook for 3 minutes and then turn and cook for a further 1 minute on the other side. Remove the fish from the pan and place skin side up on a tray.

to serve:

Arrange a small pile of spring greens onto a plate. Using a fish slice, place a warm mackerel fillet on each. Spoon the dressing around and serve immediately.

PREPARATION TIME: 15 MINS +
30 MINS FREEZING TIME

COOKING TIME: 5 MINS

Morston Hall crab cakes

BY GALTON BLACKISTON

INGREDIENTS

8 dressed crabs
2 egg yolks, beaten
4 tbsp chopped coriander
seasoned plain flour, for coating
1 egg, beaten with 75ml milk
175g white breadcrumbs

dressing:
reserved dark crab meat
splash sunflower oil
juice ½ lime
1 tsp anchovy essence
1 tbsp crème fraîche
freshly ground black pepper,
    for seasoning

to serve:
splash of olive oil
knob of butter
1 avocado, chopped
juice 1 lime
1 tbsp coriander, chopped
8 quality vine tomatoes, skinned
    and deseeded

INSTRUCTIONS

1. Using your fingers, separate the crab meat, removing any bits of shell and flaking the white meat. Reserve the dark crab meat.
2. In a bowl, combine the white crab meat with the beaten egg yolks and the coriander. Season to taste.
3. Divide the mixture into 8 and, using your hands, form 8 even-sized crab cakes. Place them on a tray and freeze for 30 minutes to firm the mixture up.
4. Meanwhile, put the seasoned flour, egg wash and breadcrumbs into separate bowls.
5. Remove the crab cakes from the freezer. Dip each crab cake into the seasoned flour to cover, then into the egg wash, shaking off any excess flour and egg wash as you go. Finally, dip each one into the breadcrumbs, making sure they are lightly and evenly coated.
6. Place the finished crab cakes on a tray lined with greaseproof paper, cover with cling film and keep in the fridge until needed.

dressing:
1. Place the dark crab meat, a splash of sunflower oil, the lime juice, anchovy essence and crème fraîche in a food processor and whiz on high speed until smooth, then taste and season.
2. Transfer to a bowl and refrigerate until needed.

to serve:
1. To cook the crab cakes, heat a large, heavy-based frying pan over a medium heat and, once hot, add a splash of olive oil together with a knob of butter. Fry the crab cakes gently for about 4 minutes on each side until they are golden.
2. Mix the chopped avocado with the juice of a lime and a tablespoon of coriander, together with skinned and deseeded vine tomatoes.
3. Put a large spoonful of the avocado mix onto a plate and arrange the crab cakes on top. Drizzle with the dressing and serve.

These crab cakes are a protein-rich light lunch, offering both omega-3 fats and selenium. They would be perfect served with a green salad.

PREPARATION TIME: 30 MINS

COOKING TIME: 2 MINS

Salad of organic salmon with carrot, coconut and lime dressing

BY SIMON BOYLE

INGREDIENTS

500g extremely fresh organic salmon
 fillet, skinned and trimmed
50g fine salt
50g caster sugar

dressing:
3 limes
1 small red chilli
1 tbsp water
1 tsp cornflour
1 medium carrot
50ml coconut milk
1 tbsp light soy sauce
1 tsp sesame oil
5 tbsp hempseed oil
freshly ground white pepper
1 bunch fresh coriander

garnish:
½ papaya
½ mango
2 spring onions
1 small chilli
coriander leaves

INSTRUCTIONS

1. Trim any brown flesh away from the salmon, season well with the salt and sugar and leave to cure for an hour.
2. After the hour, wash and dry the salmon under cold running water.
3. Slice into half centimetre slices and place on the serving plates.
4. Zest and juice the limes, de-seed the chilli and finely slice. Place in a small pan with water and bring to the boil. Dissolve the cornflour in a touch of water and stir into the lime juice, stirring until it thickens. Pour into a blender.
5. Place the carrot into a juicer, blitz and pour into a blender with the thickened lime juice.
6. Place all the other dressing ingredients into the blender and blitz until smooth.
7. Peel, de-seed and stone the papaya and mango and cut into a very neat dice, reserve until needed.
8. Half an hour before serving, take out the salmon. Whisk up the dressing and spoon over the cut fish, mix well ensuring the fish is well dressed, or serve in a small shot glass.
9. Sprinkle the fruit over the salmon along with finely sliced spring onion, chilli and coriander leaves.

Curing the salmon in this way will help to retain all of its nutritional properties, including vitamin D, heart-healthy omega-3 fats and some B-vitamins.

SERVES 2

PREPARATION TIME: 10 MINS

COOKING TIME: 10 MINS

Crostini with sun blushed tomatoes, black olives and anchovies

BY MARK JORDAN

INGREDIENTS

2 slices of fresh bread, granary or whole meal

olive oil

1 small clove garlic

100g sun blushed tomatoes

10 plump black Greek olives

1 shallot

chopped chives

8-10 fillets fresh cured anchovies

2 leaves fresh basil

INSTRUCTIONS

1. Slice the bread thinly, brush with the olive oil, rub with the garlic and place onto a tray in a medium hot oven for 10 minutes. Remove from the oven and allow to cool.

2. Using a sharp knife, roughly chop the sun blushed tomatoes and the black olives. This can be done all together. Place into a bowl.

3. Chop the garlic and the shallots nice and fine and mix with the olives and tomatoes. Mix this all well together, add a little olive oil and finally the chopped chives.

4. Take the toasted bread and spoon a good amount of the tomato and olive mix onto each slice and then arrange a couple of anchovy fillets on top with sliced basil. Serve straight away.

This easy recipe includes three cancer-fighting ingredients; tomatoes, oily fish and the allium vegetables shallots, chives and garlic.

SERVES
4

Avocado and pasta salad with flaxseed

BY SIMON BOYLE

PREPARATION TIME: 10 MINS

COOKING TIME: 15 MINS

INGREDIENTS

200g penne pasta
½ clove garlic
1 large red chilli
½ red onion
freshly ground black pepper
½ tsp Maille Dijon mustard
20ml sherry vinegar
2 limes, zested and juiced
1 tbsp wheat germ, crushed
10ml hempseed oil
1 ripe avocado

INSTRUCTIONS

1. Cook the pasta according to the packet instructions. Strain and place under running water until completely cold. Drain well in a colander.
2. Crush the garlic and place into a small mixing bowl.
3. Finely chop the red chilli and red onion and add to the garlic, season with pepper.
4. Spoon in the mustard, vinegar, lime zest, juice and wheat germ. Mix well with a whisk.
5. Pour in the hempseed oil and whisk again.
6. Cut the avocado into two and remove the stone. Using a dessert spoon, scoop out the inside (trying to do it in one go), throw away the skin. Cut the avocado into large chunks and place into the dressing to avoid discolouring.
7. Mix the pasta and avocado together with the dressing, season to taste and serve with a tomato salad.

This is a high-energy, nutrient-rich meal that is quick and easy to prepare and therefore perfect for days when you are feeling fatigued.

PREPARATION TIME: 25 MINS

COOKING TIME: 20 MINS

Grilled tuna with pineapple salsa in a honey and hempseed bap

BY SIMON BOYLE

INGREDIENTS

100ml seasoned rice vinegar

2 spring onions, finely chopped

1 tbsp Dijon mustard

¼ tsp crushed red pepper flakes

50ml extra virgin olive oil

4 x 150g fresh tuna steaks, about
    3cm thick

salsa:

1 medium fresh red chilli

1 tbsp seasoned rice vinegar

1 small fresh pineapple, very ripe

1 small red bell pepper

½ red onion

handful fresh coriander

3 tbsp olive oil

freshly ground black pepper,
    for seasoning

4 honey and hempseed baps

INSTRUCTIONS

1. In a shallow bowl, combine the vinegar, spring onions, mustard, pepper flakes and olive oil.
2. Coat the tuna with marinade and marinate refrigerated for several hours if possible, turning occasionally.

pineapple salsa:

1. Cut the chilli into 2 lengths and discard the seeds, finely chop and soak in the rice wine vinegar.
2. Peel and dice the pineapple, discarding the inner core and place into a large non-aluminum bowl.
3. Finely dice the red pepper and red onion and add to the pineapple.
4. Chop the coriander and add to the pineapple along with the chilli, vinegar and olive oil. Mix well and adjust the seasoning. Refrigerate until ready to serve.

to serve:

1. Remove the tuna from the refrigerator 30 minutes before cooking.
2. Put the baps on a low heat in the oven to warm.
3. Heat a grill pan until extremely hot. Grill the tuna 4-5 minutes per side for rare to medium-rare.
4. Serve on the warmed baps with a good spoon of salsa.

Fresh tuna steaks, unlike tinned tuna, are a good source of omega-3 fats. In this recipe tuna is paired with pineapple, an excellent source of manganese and vitamin C, to make a nutrient-packed light lunch.

Honey and hempseed baps

MAKES 8

PREPARATION TIME: 1 HR

COOKING TIME: 15 MINS

INGREDIENTS

325g strong white flour
325g strong wholemeal flour
1 tsp flaked natural sea salt
14g dried yeast
1 tbsp hempseed oil
400-450ml very warm water,
   3 parts boiling – 1 part cold
2 tsp Manuka honey
3 tbsp hemp seeds, crushed
1 egg, whisked

INSTRUCTIONS

1. In a warm bowl mix the flours, sea salt and yeast.
2. Add the oil, water, honey and half the crushed hemps seeds, mix to a soft dough. Knead for 10 minutes on a floured surface.
3. Place in a floured bowl and cover with a damp towel. Prove for at least 15 minutes or until doubled in size. Lightly knead once again on a floured surface.
4. Divide into 8 balls and place on baking sheets. Flatten with your hand by pressing the top down a little.
5. Cover and leave to rise in a warm place for 15 minutes or until doubled in size.
6. Egg wash the surface of the loaves or rolls and sprinkle with hemp seeds.
7. Place in the middle of a pre-heated oven at 230°C for 15 minutes.
8. Remove from the oven and onto a wire rack.

"Eating well during and after your treatment can help you to tolerate the treatment, accelerate your recovery afterwards, reduce your risk of the cancer returning and improve your general health and well-being."

Kelly McCabe BSc RD

Warren Goldswain/www.shutterstock.com

SERVES 2

PREPARATION TIME: 15 MINS

COOKING TIME: 20 MINS

Pepperade salad
BY MARK JORDAN

INGREDIENTS

200g pasta tubes
1 red pepper
1 yellow pepper
150ml tomato juice
10 black olives, halved and stoned
cooked fine beans
handful of pea shoots for garnish

INSTRUCTIONS

1. Boil the pasta in water until cooked, approximately 10 minutes.
2. Cut the peppers in half and remove the seeds, drizzle with oil and place onto an oven tray skin side up. Place under a grill and cook until the skin is a dark roasted colour, about 10 minutes.
3. Once the peppers are ready, remove from the grill and cling film the whole tray so that the peppers self-steam themselves. Leave for another 10 minutes. Remove the cling film and using your fingers, peel off the skin of the peppers and cut into strips.
4. Place the tomato juice and the peppers into a bowl, add the cooked pasta, the black olives and fine beans and mix well together.

to serve:
Place into a serving bowl, scatter the pea shoots around the dish and serve.

This colourful, flavoursome lunch is easy to prepare and packed full of lycopene, beta-carotene and vitamin C. To increase the nutritional value of the dish further try using whole-wheat pasta.

PREPARATION TIME: 48 HRS IN
ADVANCE TO SOUSE MACKEREL
+ 30 MINS ON THE DAY

Soused mackerel, beetroot and pickled cucumber

BY PETER FIORI

INGREDIENTS

4 mackerel fillets, deboned

pickled cucumber:
37.5ml white wine vinegar
50g caster sugar
50ml water
½ cucumber, sliced into half moons
2 sprigs dill

marinade:
300ml white wine vinegar
100g caster sugar
125g sliced onion
1 bay leaf
5 crushed peppercorns
1 all spice berries
sprigs of thyme, chopped

horseradish cream:
100g low fat crème fraîche
40g horseradish sauce
juice ¼ lemon

beetroot relish:
150g beetroot, cooked and diced
15g low fat crème fraîche
½ tbsp horseradish cream
½ tsp grated horseradish
juice ¼ lemon

INSTRUCTIONS

pickled cucumber:
1. Bring the vinegar, sugar and water to a boil and allow to cool.
2. Peel the cucumber, cut lengthways, remove the seeds and slice thinly.
3. Mix the cucumber with the chopped dill and pickle in the cooled mix for 30 minutes.

marinade:
1. Bring all the marinade ingredients to the boil and leave to cool.
2. When cool, put the fillets of mackerel in the marinade and leave to souse for 2 days.

horseradish cream:
Mix all the ingredients together.

beetroot relish:
Mix all the ingredients together.

to serve:
Place the beetroot relish on the base of the plate, lay the drained mackerel fillet on top. Finish with the cucumber pickle. Dot the plate with the horseradish cream.

Sousing is an interesting method of pickling fish without needing to cure the fish through the addition of salt or smoke. It gives a wonderful vinegary flavour to the dish. This method would be useful for people who have a heightened sense of smell during and after treatment as you avoid the strong cooking smell of fish.

PREPARATION TIME: 10 MINS

COOKING TIME: 15 MINS

INGREDIENTS

200g middle cut tuna loin
vegetable oil
100g Jersey royals
1 shallot
mayonnaise
chopped chives
2 whole tomatoes

to serve:
10 fine beans
8 tomato petals
10 fillets of anchovies
10 black olives
1 punnet cress
basil oil

Mark Jordan's tuna nicoise
BY MARK JORDAN

INSTRUCTIONS

1. Start by searing the tuna. Place some vegetable oil in a non-stick frying pan and allow to heat up. Place the tuna loin into the pan and cook on each side for about 1 minute, the tuna should should still be raw in the middle. Once all sides are sealed, wrap the tuna tightly in cling film and place in the fridge to cool down and set up.
2. Boil the potatoes until cooked, dice and add the chopped shallot to them. Add a couple of spoons of mayonnaise and mix gently together, sprinkling in some chopped chives.
3. Place a small cut into the top of the tomatoes and plunge into boiling water for 8 seconds and then place into ice cold water to remove the skin. Cut the tomatoes into quarters and remove the seeds, cut the flesh into strips.

to serve:
1. Place a spoonful of potato salad onto the centre of a plate.
2. Remove the tuna from the fridge and slice with a sharp knife and sit on top of the potato salad.
3. Cook the beans in boiling water for 2 minutes.
4. Arrange the tomato petals around the dish along with the anchovies, fine beans and the black olives.
5. Garnish with the cress and a little drizzle of basil oil serve straight away.

This twist on a traditional nicoise salad uses fresh tuna steak which is an excellent source of omega-3 fatty acids and lean protein. If you don't have basil oil at home use a good quality olive oil instead. Basil-infused oil can be made fairly easily at home by blending fresh basil leaves with olive oil and warming over a low heat before straining and leaving to cool.

PREPARATION TIME: 50 MINS + 4 HRS
TO MARINADE THE QUAIL

COOKING TIME: 40 MINS

Roast quail with spiced vegetables
BY PETER FIORI

INGREDIENTS

4 qualis

quail marinade:
2 cloves crushed garlic
1 tsp rock salt
30ml olive oil
juice 1 lemon
1 tbsp chopped thyme
1½ tsp ground turmeric
1½ tsp freshly ground black pepper
1 tsp ground coriander

spiced vegetables:
3 baby artichokes
150g peeled pumpkin wedges
16 peeled baby carrot halves
6 shallot halves
16 peeled baby turnip halves
200g sweet potato 2cm dice
2 tsp crushed coriander seeds
½ tsp freshly ground black pepper
30 leaves fresh chopped mint
3 tbsp olive oil
pinch saffron
500ml water
juice 1 lemon
30 leaves fresh chopped tarragon
120g broad beans shelled
60g frozen or fresh peas
100g green beans

INSTRUCTIONS

marinade:
Mix all the marinade ingredients together.

quails:
1. Ask your butcher to spatchcock the quails. Skewer the birds.
2. Marinate the quails for 4 hours.
3. Heat a chargrill and colour the quails for 3 minutes each side, place on a tray and cook at 180°C for 12 minutes, rest for 5 minutes before serving.

spiced vegetables:
1. Trim the artichokes and cut into quarters. Mix with the pumpkin, carrot, shallot, turnip and sweet potato.
2. Add the spices, chopped mint and olive oil and mix until thoroughly coated.
3. Heat a thick bottom frying pan and sauté until the vegetables are golden brown.
4. Transfer to a casserole pan and add the saffron, water, lemon juice and tarragon leaves and simmer gently for approximately 25 minutes until tender.
5. Whilst the vegetables are cooking, blanch the broad beans in boiling water for 30 seconds and refresh in iced water. Drain and remove the shells.
6. Add the peas, green beans and broad beans and cook for a further 10 minutes.
7. Serve warm with the quail.

The olive oil and ground black pepper in this marinade have been found to aid the absorption of curcumin, the active ingredient in turmeric, which has been shown to have anti-inflammatory and anti-oxidant properties. Try adding oil and pepper each time you use turmeric.

PREPARATION TIME: 45 MINS

COOKING TIME: 3-4 MINS
FOR LOBSTER TAILS

Lobster salad with sweet and sour dressing, mooli and ginger

BY JASON ATHERTON

INGREDIENTS

2 medium uncooked Scottish
    lobster tails
¼ large or ½ small mooli (Japanese
    radish)
olive oil, to glaze

sweet and sour dressing:
60ml sherry vinegar
140g thick honey
300ml groundnut oil

to serve:
crushed ginger
freshly ground black pepper,
    for serving

INSTRUCTIONS

lobster:

1. Bring a pan of salted water to the boil. Uncurl the lobster tails and place them together, head to tail end with their flesh sides touching. Secure with kitchen string. This will ensure the the tails do not curl up when cooking.
2. Add the tails to the pan and poach for 3-4 minutes or until cooked through. Remove from the water and leave to cool slightly. Use a pair of kitchen scissors to snip along the bottom shell of each lobster tail. Prise the shells apart to release the flesh. Wrap the lobster meat in cling film and chill until ready to use.
3. Peel the mooli and slice lengthways into wafer-thin slices using a mandoline. Stack the mooli slices and use a small round cutter 5-6 cm in diameter, to stamp out neat discs.

sweet and sour dressing:

1. Combine the ingredients in a wide bowl and stir until evenly blended.
2. Add the mooli slices one at a time, ensuring that each disc is well coated with dressing before adding another. Cover the bowl with cling film and chill for 30 minutes.

to serve:

1. Place 3 marinated mooli discs on each serving plate.
2. Cut the poached lobster tails into bite-sized pieces then rub them with a little olive oil to give them a shiny appearance.
3. Place 1 or 2 pieces of lobster on each mooli disc and sprinkle with a little ginger and freshly ground black pepper.
4. Drizzle the plates with a little sweet and sour dressing and serve immediately.

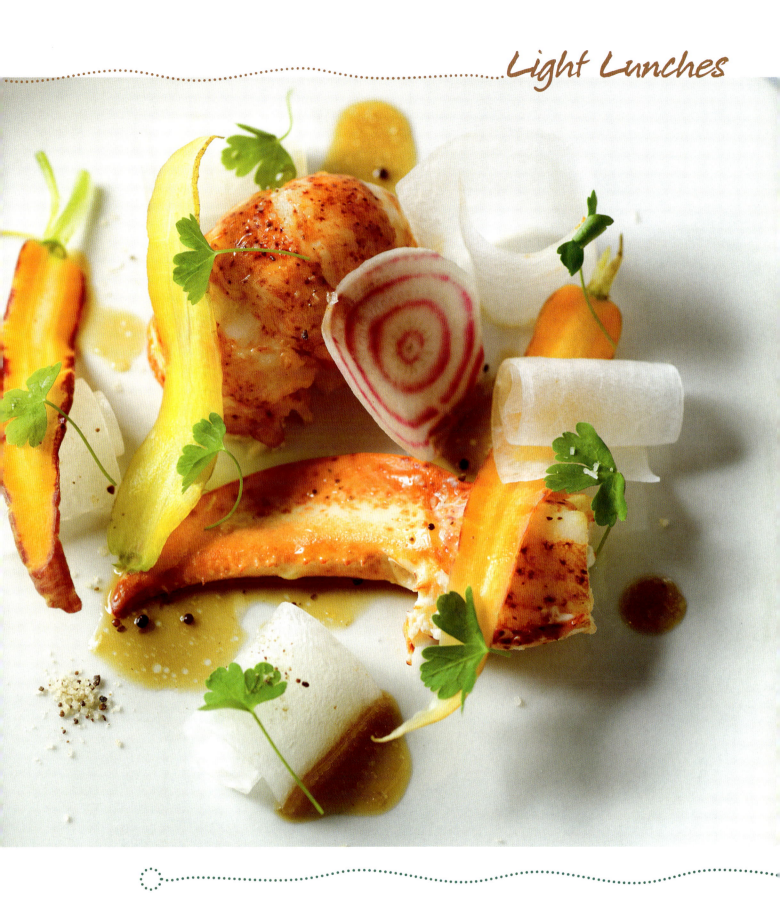

Lobster, although often considered an extravagant ingredient, is readily available and surprisingly easy to cook. This dish would make a delicious, nutritious starter for a dinner party.

103

BROCCOLI

A cruciferous vegetable

RED ONION

Mild and sweet

PREPARATION TIME: 40 MINS

COOKING TIME: 20 MINS

Grilled halibut with lemon and capers

BY JOHN WILLIAMS

INGREDIENTS

grilled halibut:
150g fillet of halibut
1½ baby artichokes
3 baby spring onions
20ml olive oil
50g cauliflower purée
1 lemon, zest, segments and juice
10g capers, superfine
1 bunch chervil, chopped
½ shallot
3 nasturtium leaves (optional)
seasoning, to taste

cauliflower purée:
½ cauliflower
50g butter
200ml cream
200ml milk
freshly ground black pepper,
    for seasoning

INSTRUCTIONS

grilled halibut:
1. Roast the halibut in the oven so the fish is just cooked.
2. Prepare the baby artichokes, removing the chokes and cooking in lemon water. Once cooked, refresh and cut in half.
3. Peel the onions leaving some of the green stalk, cook in olive oil and a little water until tender, cut in half.
4. Prepare a classic cauliflower purée (see below) and finish with a touch of butter and cream.
5. Peel the lemon zest and cut into fine julienne and remove the segments from the pith, keeping the natural shape.
6. Rinse the capers in water to remove any excess brine or salt.
7. Combine the zest and segments with the capers, chopped chervil and shallot, pour on the olive oil and the juice of the lemon.
8. Spoon a little purée onto the plate and dress the artichokes and nasturtium leaves around the fish.
9. Spoon the garnish and dressing over the top.

cauliflower purée:
1. Slice the cauliflower thinly on a mandoline
2. Get a pan hot and add the butter so that it starts to foam.
3. Add the cauliflower and cook quickly until softened.
4. Add the cream and milk to the cauliflower.
5. Cook quickly again, stirring as it reduces.
6. Once cooked, drain and purée, reserving the excess cream and milk to adjust consistency.
7. Season with pepper and pass through a chinois.

This recipe uses leaves from the edible plant, nasturtium. The entire nasturtium plant is edible including the leaves, flowers, stems and seeds. They are extremely easy to grow in your garden and make a colourful addition to salads whilst adding plenty of vitamin C and iron.

SERVES
4

PREPARATION TIME: 30-40 MINS

COOKING TIME: 10-15 MINS

Salad of baked mackerel, watermelon, beetroot and raspberry vinaigrette

BY STEVE DRAKE

INGREDIENTS

mackerel:
4 large fillets of mackerel
2 tbsp olive oil

charred watermelon:
½ watermelon
a little oil

beetroot dressing:
100g beetroot juice
dash raspberry vinegar, to taste
10 toasted and well ground
    coriander seeds
100g olive oil
50g lemon juice

beetroots:
1 bunch of baby beetroots
1 tbsp olive oil
freshly ground black pepper,
    for seasoning

to serve:
16 fresh raspberries, cut in half
small handful rainbow chard
1 tsp beetroot dressing

INSTRUCTIONS

mackerel:
1. Remove any small bones, rinse in cold water and dry the fillets.
2. Using a very sharp knife score the skin.
3. Brush the mackerel fillets with the olive oil.
4. Place on an oiled tray and bake in a very hot oven for 3-4 minutes, 200°C.

charred watermelon:
1. Slice the watermelon into 15mm slices, remove the rind and all seeds
2. Cut into batons 15x15x40mm, brush with oil and char on a griddle.

beetroot dressing:
1. Season the juice with a dash of raspberry vinegar.
2. Toast the seeds and grind, add everything else together.
3. Mix well and store in a kilner jar until needed.

beetroots:
1. Cut the stalk of the beetroots, wash in cold water and wrap in tin foil with the olive oil and seasoning.
2. Bake in the oven at 160°C for 10-15 minutes. Whilst still warm peel (wearing rubber gloves) and place in a bowl with 2 tbs of the dressing.

to serve:
1. Add the watermelon pieces to the beetroot bowl and toss. Scatter the beetroot and watermelon over 4 plates.
2. Lay the mackerel fillet on top and then the raspberries.
3. Finally dress the leaves and scatter over with a little extra dressing.

Watermelon, like tomatoes, is an extremely rich source of lycopene, and adds a refreshing twist to this mackerel salad.

Garam masala chicken wrap with mango dip

BY JOHN WILLIAMS

SERVES
1

PREPARATION TIME: 20 MINS +
2 HRS MARINATING TIME

COOKING TIME: 7 MINS

INGREDIENTS

chicken wrap:
1 medium breast of chicken
60ml low fat yoghurt
10g chopped shallot
½ lemon, juice and zest
10 leaves coriander, chopped
1 tsp finely grated ginger
½ clove garlic, chopped
pinch cinnamon
½ tsp turmeric
½ tsp curry paste
1 tortilla wrap
5 leaves coriander, to serve

mango dip:
1 mango, flesh
1 lime, juice and zest
2 tbs mango chutney
8 leaves coriander, chopped

INSTRUCTIONS

chicken wrap:
1. Cut the breast into 3 strips long ways and place into a bowl. Lightly score the meat so that the spice will penetrate.
2. Combine all the other ingredients in a bowl and mix well. Set a third of the mix aside for service and add the chicken to the remaining mix. Leave to marinate for up to one day, 2 hours will suffice.
3. Place a griddle onto a hot stove until very hot and oil well.
4. Place the marinated chicken on to the grill and cook for 2-3 minutes on each side; this can be seared in a skillet.
5. Remove and allow to rest.
6. Mix a little of the reserved yoghurt marinade with the cooked chicken and lay onto a flour tortilla. Sprinkle with coriander and roll into a wrap
7. Cut to appropriate size and serve with mango dip condiment.

mango dip:
1. Cut the flesh of the mango into 5mm dice, squeeze the lime juice and finely grated lime zest and mix with chutney and coriander.
2. Set aside to serve alongside as a condiment.

This is an easy, high-protein lunch that uses spiced low-fat yoghurt to add flavour and moisture to the chicken. This could be used as a substitute for mayonnaise in other recipes to reduce the saturated fat content.

SERVES 6

PREPARATION TIME: 15 MINS

COOKING TIME: 10 MINS

Asparagus, French beans and sugar snap peas with orange and hazelnuts

BY ANDREW FAIRLIE

INGREDIENTS

300g asparagus

300g French beans

300g sugar snap peas

80g whole hazelnuts

1 orange

1 small garlic clove, crushed

1 bunch chives

3 tbs light olive oil

2 tbs hazelnut oil

INSTRUCTIONS

1. Preheat the oven to 180°C.
2. Peel the asparagus and trim the French beans and sugar snap peas.
3. Bring a large pot of lightly salted water to a rapid boil, add the asparagus and boil for about 4 minutes or until just tender. With a slotted spoon, remove the asparagus and plunge into a bowl of iced water to stop the cooking and preserve the colour. Repeat the process for the beans and peas, but the peas will need far less cooking time. When the vegetables are thoroughly chilled pour them into a colander to drain.
4. While the beans are cooking place the hazelnuts into the oven to colour lightly. Cool and roughly chop.
5. Using a vegetable peeler or a zester, remove the zest from the orange and cut into thin strips.
6. Pat the vegetables dry, put into a large mixing bowl and add the zest, garlic, chives, hazelnuts and oils. Mix well.
7. Serve at room temperature.

Try making this incredibly healthy anti-inflammatory salad as either a light lunch or side dish. The Asparagus is a rich source of folic acid, vitamin K and vitamin A, whilst the orange adds extra vitamin C.

PREPARATION TIME: 30 MINS

COOKING TIME: 15 MINS

Poached Loch Duart salmon, black garlic mayonnaise, potato and capers

BY STEVE DRAKE

INGREDIENTS

salmon:
1 litre water
100ml dry white wine
1 star anise
1 bay leaf
1½ small onion, chopped
¼ bulb fennel, chopped
1 small carrot, chopped
400g piece of Loch Duart salmon

black garlic mayonnaise:
50g black garlic
10g Chardonnay vinegar
20g water
1 egg
250ml sunflower oil

to serve:
400g Jersey Royals
2 tbsp fried capers
4 tbsp black garlic mayonnaise

INSTRUCTIONS

salmon:
1. Place all the ingredients in a narrow pan except the fish and bring to the boil. Allow to simmer for 5 minutes.
2. Remove the pan from the heat and add the fish leaving to gently cook in the residual heat for 8-12 minutes.
3. Remove from the stock onto a warm plate and cover.

black garlic mayonnaise:
1. Place all the ingredients in a tall narrow jug, except the oil.
2. Using a hand blender with the blade attachment purée until smooth and then slowly pour in the oil to form the mayonnaise.

to serve:
3. Cook the Jersey Royals in boiling salted water until just cooked, drain the water and keep warm in the pan.
4. Take 50g of capers in brine, drain them and lay on kitchen paper to absorb the brine and fry at 180°C until the buds have popped open and crispy.
5. Cut the potatoes in half and place cut side down on the plates, flake the salmon over the top, adding a few blobs of the black garlic mayonnaise, finally scatter the capers over the top.

Loch Duart Salmon is farmed in Northern Scotland using safe, sustainable techniques without the use of artificial dyes or additives. If you cannot find Loch Duart Salmon try to buy wild salmon instead.

PREPARATION TIME: 25 MINS

COOKING TIME: 8-10 MINS

Steamed white asparagus with flat parsley and boiled egg vinaigrette

BY DANIEL GALMICHE

INGREDIENTS

500g white asparagus (or green)

2-3 litres water

vinaigrette:

2 eggs, boiled and chopped

2 tsp Dijon mustard

2 tbsp white wine vinegar

freshly ground black pepper

100ml sunflower or olive oil

small handful of fresh chopped parsley

INSTRUCTIONS

1. If the asparagus is fresh and young, you do not need to peel it, if not you do. Cut or snap off the ends. Bring 2 saucepans of water to the boil, 1 small for the eggs and 1 larger for the asparagus.

2. Boil the eggs for 10 minutes.

3. Before you drop the asparagus in, you should tie it up loosely with string, the tips all facing the same way.

4. Place them in the water and reduce to a low heat. Cook for 6-10 minutes according to the size of your asparagus.

5. While they are cooking, put the mustard, vinegar and pepper in a bowl, mix well and slowly add the oil.

6. When the eggs are ready, peel and them and add them to the vinaigrette together with the flat parsley.

7. Prepare a bowl of ice cold water for blanching. To check if the asparagus is ready gently pierce with a knife; it should go in easily but still be quite firm. Remove and plunge into the ice cold water. This helps to keep the chlorophyll and therefore the goodness and colour locked in.

8. Serve on a flat dish and pour over the vinaigrette.

Research has shown that people who consume eggs for breakfast eat approximately 400 calories less throughout the day. The remarkable ability of eggs to keep us feeling full makes them perfect for a light lunch that will keep you going until dinner time.

SERVES
4

PREPARATION TIME: 40 MINS

COOKING TIME: 10 MINS

Grilled fillet of salmon with green apple salad, ginger and lime dressing

BY ANDREW FAIRLIE

INGREDIENTS

chicken:

4 salmon fillets

2 Granny Smith apples, cut into matchsticks

2 spring onions, thinly sliced

1 small red onion, thinly sliced

small bunch fresh mint leaves

small bunch fresh coriander leaves

juice of 2 limes

100g roasted cashew nuts

ginger dressing:

50g grated palm sugar

2 tbs fish sauce

2 tbs grated fresh ginger

INSTRUCTIONS

1. Rinse the salmon gently under cold water and pat dry.
2. Combine the ingredients for the ginger dressing in a small saucepan, bring to a boil, remove from the heat, strain and cool.
3. Place the salmon onto a grill tray and cook under a hot grill until just cooked.
4. Combine the apples, onions, mint, coriander and lime juice in a mixing bowl, pour over some of the dressing and toss lightly.
5. Divide the fish onto serving plates, garnish with the salad. Sprinkle cashews on top and drizzle a little of the remaining dressing around the fish.

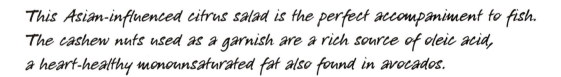

This Asian-influenced citrus salad is the perfect accompaniment to fish.
The cashew nuts used as a garnish are a rich source of oleic acid,
a heart-healthy monounsaturated fat also found in avocados.

PREPARATION TIME: 35 MINS

COOKING TIME: 20 MINS

Grilled chicken breast with lentil salad

BY DANIEL GALMICHE

INGREDIENTS

chicken:

4 chicken breasts, free range,
   medium sized with skin on
freshly ground black pepper,
   for seasoning
olive oil, for seasoning

lentils:

200g lentils (preferably Le Puy)
1 shallot, whole, peeled
1 small carrot, diced
1 bouquet garni (thyme & parsley only)
1 clove garlic, skin on
French vinaigrette
a handful of chervil, chopped
freshly ground black pepper,
   for seasoning

INSTRUCTIONS

grilled chicken breast:

1. Take the chicken breast, place in a small dish and season with the pepper and olive oil. Leave to marinate for a few minutes

2. Preheat the oven at 200°C. Place a grill pan on a medium heat and grill skin side down for 5 minutes, then turn the other side and do the same for another 5 minutes. When ready and properly marked but not burnt, place in an oven dish and cook in the oven for a further 10 minutes.

lentils:

3. Rinse the lentils thoroughly as there can be tiny stones in them, no bigger than the lentils themselves – it's rare but worth checking for. Put them in a small pan and cover with cold water.

4. Bring to the boil and skim the white foam from the surface.

5. Add the whole shallot, carrot, bouquet garni and garlic and simmer for a further 10 minutes until al dente.

6. Drain, keeping 2 tablespoons of cooking liquid aside, remove the shallot, the bouquet garni and garlic but leave the carrots in.

7. Add the vinaigrette, the remaining cooking liquid and fresh chervil. Check the seasoning and this should give you a lovely lentil salad.

to serve:

Put a generous spoonful of lentils into the middle of a plate and place a chicken breast on top, grilled side up.

If cooking this recipe regularly, ensure you remove the skin from the chicken breasts. This will significantly reduce the saturated fat content and caloric value of the dish.

SERVES 4

SERVES 4 SMALL MEALS OR 2 MAIN

PREPARATION TIME: 20 MINS

COOKING TIME: 7 MINS

Chargrilled beef salad

BY ANDREW FAIRLIE

INGREDIENTS

500g thick sirloin steak, fat removed

60ml fish sauce

60ml lime juice

1 tsp light soy sauce

1 tbsp grated palm sugar

1 clove garlic, crushed

3 Lebanese cucumbers, seeded
   and sliced

2 small red Thai chillies

8 large green spring onions

250g red cherry tomatoes

1 head baby gem lettuce

1 small bunch mint leaves

1 small bunch coriander leaves

INSTRUCTIONS

1. Marinate the beef in 2 tablespoons of the fish sauce and 1 tablespoon of the lime juice, place into a bowl and leave for 3 hours or even overnight in the fridge.

2. Drain the beef, discard any remaining marinade. Chargrill the beef on a grill plate or BBQ until cooked rare. Leave to rest.

3. Meanwhile, combine the remaining fish sauce, lime juice, soy sauce, palm sugar and garlic in a screw top jar, shake well.

4. Mix the cucumber, chilli, onions, tomatoes, lettuce and herbs, season with the dressing and gently toss to combine.

5. Place the salad onto serving plates, thinly slice the still warm beef and arrange over the salad.

In this recipe three techniques are used which, if copied at home, could help to make your barbecues safer; 1. the meat is marinated overnight before cooking, 2. the fat is removed before cooking 3. the meat is cooked over the griddle for only a short time (for white meats which cannot be eaten rare, it is advisable to briefly pre-cook them in an oven).

SERVES
8

PREPARATION TIME: 15 MINS

COOKING TIME: 40 MINS

Camargue red rice and quinoa salad with pistachios, orange and rocket

BY ANDREW FAIRLIE

INGREDIENTS

60g shelled pistachios
200g quinoa
200g Camargue red rice
1 medium onion, sliced
150ml olive oil
grated zest and juice of 1 orange
2 tsp lemon juice
1 garlic clove crushed
4 spring onions sliced thinly
100g dried apricots roughly chopped
100g rocket
freshly ground black pepper,
    for seasoning
wholemeal pitta bread, to serve

INSTRUCTIONS

1. Place the pistachios onto a tray and place under a hot grill and lightly toast, cool and chop roughly.
2. Fill 2 saucepans with lightly salted water and bring to a boil. Cook the quinoa in one for approximately 14 minutes until just cooked, but still have a bite to it. Cook the rice in the other pan for 20 minutes, again until just cooked.
3. When both are cooked drain in a colander and spread out onto a tray to cool down.
4. Whilst the grains are cooking, cook the sliced onion in 4 tablespoons of the olive oil until golden. Cool completely.
5. In a large mixing bowl, combine the grains, onions and the remaining oil, mix gently. Add the rest of the ingredients and season.
6. Serve with some warm wholemeal pitta bread.

This dish includes two gluten-free wholegrains, Quinoa and Red Rice. Both are rich in protein, iron and fibre. Camargue red rice, grown in Southern France, has a nutty taste and a chewy texture. It is much richer in fibre, B-vitamins and minerals than white rice and is much more filling, meaning you can have smaller portions.

Soup

All of the soups in this section provide a nutritious, comforting alternative to a cooked meal for times when you are feeling tired or you lack time to prepare a complex dish. Keeping supplies of home-made soups in your freezer will mean you always have a healthy meal to hand.

Soup often becomes a dietary staple during cancer treatment, particularly if people are experiencing taste changes, a sore mouth or swallowing difficulties. Soups also contribute to daily fluid intake, helping you to keep well hydrated.

All of the soups in this section could be used both during, and after cancer treatment. They have been selected because they include a variety of cancer fighting nutrients such as kombu, an iodine rich seaweed that can be purchased from Asian food stores, or beetroot which contains the phytochemical beta-cyanin, found to be protective against colon cancer. Or why not make a batch of the spiced split pea soup as research has shown that including one portion of pulses, such as lentils or beans, in your diet each day can help to stabilise blood glucose levels due to their high soluble fibre content.

Butternut squash and sweet potato soup with roasted pumpkin seeds

BY MARK JORDAN

PREPARATION TIME: **20 MINS +
OVERNIGHT FOR INFUSION**

COOKING TIME: **20 MINS**

INGREDIENTS

1 butternut squash
1 sweet potato
1 pt chicken stock
1 pt soya milk
pepper, for seasoning
pumpkin seeds
chopped chives

curry oil:
a little vegetable oil
1 tsp curry powder

INSTRUCTIONS

1. Peel both the butternut squash and the sweet potato and cut into a smallish dice, place into a saucepan, add the chicken stock and bring to the boil.
2. Simmer the soup for about 20 minutes or until the vegetables are very soft. At this point add half of the soya milk and place into a blender. Purée until silky smooth, pass through a fine sieve and adjust the seasoning.
3. Place the pumpkin seeds onto a lightly oiled tray and place into a medium-hot oven until golden brown.

curry oil:
Gently heat up a little vegetable oil and add 1 teaspoon of curry powder and leave to infuse over night. Pass through a fine cloth and reserve.

to serve:
1. Place the soup back into a saucepan and bring to a boil. Using a stick blender aerate the soup and then pour into the serving dishes.
2. Sprinkle a few of the roasted pumpkin seeds on top with a drizzle of the curry oil, a few chopped chives and serve straight away.

SERVES 4

PREPARATION TIME: 20 MINS

COOKING TIME: 25 MINS

Celeriac and apple soup

BY SAM MOODY

INGREDIENTS

1 shallot, peeled and sliced

1 garlic clove

50ml olive oil

500g celeriac

300g milk

400g water

1 apple, Granny Smith or Cox's

small bunch chives, chopped

good olive oil and cracked black
pepper to finish

INSTRUCTIONS

1. In a wide heavy based pan sweat the shallot and garlic for about 5 minutes in the olive oil .
2. Peel and dice the celeriac into small cubes, add to the sweated shallots and cook for 10 minutes.
3. Add the milk and water, bring to a simmer and cook out for 10 minutes.
4. Once cooked, blend to a smooth soup in a food processor.
5. Grate a Granny Smith apple, dress with a little olive oil, and chopped chives.
6. Place the apple into the middle of the soup bowl and pour over the hot celeriac soup.
7. Finish with a drizzle of good olive oil and a pinch of pepper.

CABBAGE

Adds crunch to your salads

BEET

Sweet and earthy

PREPARATION TIME: 20 MINS

COOKING TIME: 40-50 MINS

Beetroot soup with creme fraiche and goat's cheese

BY JASON ATHERTON

INGREDIENTS

500g beetroot (4 large ones)
1½ tbsp olive oil
1 large shallot, peeled and chopped
1 clove garlic
splash of balsamic vinegar
1 litre chicken stock
few thyme sprigs, leaves only
freshly ground black pepper,
   for seasoning

to serve:
100g crème fraîche
50g soft goat's cheese (optional)

INSTRUCTIONS

1. Peel and finely chop the beetroot.
2. Heat the olive oil in a medium-large saucepan. Add the shallot and garlic and cook, stirring frequently over a medium heat for 5-6 minutes until the shallot is soft. Tip in the beetroot. Stir well and cook over a high heat for another 5 minutes. Deglaze the pan with a splash of balsamic vinegar and let it boil dry.
3. Pour in the chicken stock and add the thyme leaves. Bring to the boil, reduce the heat and simmer for about 40-50 minutes or until the beetroot is very soft.
4. While still hot, transfer the beetroot to a blender or food processor using a slotted spoon. Pour in some of the stock and blend until smooth. Pass the mixture through a fine sieve into a clean pan. Stir in more of the stock until you reach the desired consistency. Season with pepper to taste. Reheat the soup if serving hot, or if serving cold allow to cool down for a few hours.
5. Beat the crème fraîche and goat's cheese together in a bowl until smooth. Pour the soup into individual bowls and drop in a spoonful of crème fraîche.

Vegetable broth

BY JOHN WILLIAMS

**SERVES
8-10**

PREPARATION TIME: 30 MINS

COOKING TIME: 40 MINS

INGREDIENTS

1 large onion
2 garlic cloves, finely chopped
50g butter
50ml olive oil
1 swede
2 carrots
1 large potato
¼ celeriac
2 courgettes
1 leek
1 bouquet garni
4 Litre vegetable stock or
    chicken stock
50g peas, blanched
50g French beans, thinly sliced
50g broad beans
5g chopped parsley
5g chopped chives

INSTRUCTIONS

1. Chop the onion and slowly sweat off with the garlic in the butter and oil, no colouring required.
2. Finely chop all the vegetables in a uniform dice, approximately 5mm square, keeping each vegetable separate.
3. Once the onion has softened, add the swede, carrot, potato and celeriac.
4. Cook for 5-10 minutes then add the courgettes, leek and bouquet garni.
5. Cook for a further 4 minutes then add the stock, just to cover.
6. Simmer until all the vegetables are tender.
7. Finish with the blanched peas and beans and finally the chopped herbs.
8. Season to taste.

SERVES 4

PREPARATION TIME: 10 MINS

COOKING TIME: 30 MINS

Spiced split yellow pea soup
BY SAM MOODY

INGREDIENTS

1 shallot
1 garlic clove
1 chili
10g fresh ginger
50ml olive oil
1 tsp curry powder
200g yellow lentils
500g water

to serve:
1 tbsp yoghurt

INSTRUCTIONS

1. Chop the shallot, garlic, chilli, and ginger. Heat the oil in a wide heavy based pan and add. Cook over a medium heat for 5 minutes, colouring lightly.
2. Add the curry powder and cook for a further 2 minutes, now add the lentils, mix well then add the water. Simmer for 20-30 minutes.
3. Once the peas are soft, blitz with a hand blender, serve with yoghurt and freshly chopped coriander.

SERVES
4

PREPARATION TIME: 45 MINS

COOKING TIME: 10-15 MINS

INGREDIENTS

kombu water:
100g kombu sheets
1 litre water

broccoli soup:
4 heads broccoli
1 litre kombu water

girolle mushrooms:
100g fresh wild girolle mushrooms
1 tbsp olive oil
freshly ground black pepper,
    for seasoning

garnish:
borage flowers

Broccoli and Kombu soup with girolle mushrooms and Borage flowers

BY STEVE DRAKE

INSTRUCTIONS

kombu water:
1. Soak the kombu in the water for 30 minutes and then put on to boil. Just as it starts to boil, remove from the heat and remove the kombu sheets, these have now done their job and can be discarded.
2. Allow to cool or use immediately.

broccoli soup:
1. Cut the broccoli heads into florets.
2. Bring the kombu water to the boil and add the broccoli florets.
3. Boil rapidly for 4 minutes only and whilst hot pour into a blender.
4. Blend until smooth.
5. Add a little seasoning to taste if needed.
6. Cool quickly to avoid discolouration and chill to be reheated later.

girolle mushrooms:
Briefly clean the mushrooms ready for cooking.

to finish:
1. Heat the soup in a sauce pan and pour into warm bowls.
2. Heat 1 tablespoon of olive oil in a small frying pan, add the girolles and cook for 1 minute, adding a little pepper to taste.
3. Drain onto some kitchen paper and sprinkle onto the soup.
4. Finally lay your borage flowers on top.

Main Meals

PREPARATION TIME: 25 MINS

COOKING TIME: 25 MINS

INGREDIENTS

dressing:
10 fresh raspberries
40ml red wine vinegar
1 shallot
50g semi dried figs
½ tsp grain mustard
1 tbsp Manuka honey
freshly ground black pepper,
    for seasoning
100ml hempseed oil

poached beef:
6 yellow (or red) baby plum tomatoes
1 clove garlic
1 sprig thyme
1 tbsp extra virgin olive oil
1 litre beef stock
800g whole beef fillet, tied 2-3 times
1 small Savoy cabbage

Poached beef fillet with semi dried figs and raspberry vinaigrette

BY SIMON BOYLE

INSTRUCTIONS

dressing:
1. Crush the raspberries with a fork and steep in the red wine vinegar.
2. Peel and finely chop the shallot and cut the figs into wedges, add to the raspberries and mix in the grain mustard. Season with the honey and pepper and stir in the hempseed oil. Reserve.

poached beef:
1. Cut the tomatoes in half and place in a bowl.
2. Crush the garlic and pull the leaves from the thyme. Mix with the tomatoes and drizzle with olive oil. Season and place on an oven tray and roast in a hot oven for 5 minutes. Take out and reserve.
3. Bring the beef stock to a gentle simmer in a wide pan and keep it simmering over a low-medium heat. Meanwhile, heat a little olive oil in a large heavy frying pan until very hot, and sear the fillet of beef over a high heat until nicely coloured on both sides. Transfer the steaks to the stock, making sure it is covered in liquid.
4. Simmer gently for 8 minutes for rare beef, 12 minutes for medium and 16 minutes for well done. Do not let the liquid boil. Remove the fillet from the stock and rest for 5 minutes.
5. While the steaks are resting, shred the Savoy cabbage fairly finely and blanch in the beef stock for 3-4 minutes only. Take out when cooked but still with a slight bite. Drain well and season with a little dressing.

to serve:
1. Place the cabbage in the centre of the plate, slice the beef equally into 4 and place on the cabbage.
2. Place the tomato halves around the plate and drizzle the dressing around.

Antioxidant-packed raspberries and figs make an unusual yet delicious accompaniment to beef in this iron-rich recipe.

SERVES 4

PREPARATION TIME: 20 MINS

COOKING TIME: 25 MINS

Chargrilled monkfish loin, Oriental broth, pak choi

BY SAM MOODY

INGREDIENTS

2 shallots
1 carrot
6 button mushrooms
2 garlic
1 chilli
10g fresh ginger
50ml sesame oil
1 tsp, dark soy sauce,
1 tsp fish sauce
400g trimmed boneless
    monkfish loin
2 heads choi
handful coriander

INSTRUCTIONS

1. Heat a wok, chop up all of vegetables, purée the garlic, chilli and ginger.
2. Add the sesame oil to the wok, add the shallots, stir fry for 2 minutes, add the chilli, garlic and ginger, cook for 2 minutes. Add the carrots and mushrooms, cook for 3 minutes.
3. Cover with hot water, add the soy and fish sauce and allow to simmer while you cook the monk fish.
4. Preheat a griddle pan and char the monkfish all around, 3-5 minutes on each side, turn off the heat and allow to rest in the pan.
5. Roughly shred the choi and add to the broth, shred a good handful of fresh coriander and add to the broth.
6. Serve into a preheated bowl, carve the monk fish and place on top.

The chilli, garlic and ginger in this recipe are a classic combination that create a delicious oriental flavour whilst adding important cancer-protective phytochemicals; capsaicin, allicin and gingerol. Try using this combination of flavours with other types of fish.

SERVES 4

PREPARATION TIME: 15 MINS

COOKING TIME: 25 MINS

Beetroot and chilli risotto

BY SIMON BOYLE

INGREDIENTS

1 small onion, finely chopped

100g unsalted butter

2 cloves garlic, chopped

1 small red chilli, deseeded and
    chopped

1 medium beetroot, peeled and grated

320g (or a mug) Arborio rice

1 tsp cumin seeds

1 tsp Garam Masala

1 glass white wine

1 litre hot vegetable stock

80g Parmesan cheese

1 handful fresh coriander, chopped

80ml crème fraîche

1 lime, zest and juiced

INSTRUCTIONS

1. In a large saucepan gently fry the finely chopped onion in half
    the butter for 1 minute or so. Add the chopped garlic and chilli
    and continue cooking until soft but not coloured.

2. Peel and grate the beetroot. Add this into the pan and continue
    cooking for a further 2-3 minutes.

3. Stir in the rice, cumin seeds and Garam Masala to the onions
    and turn the heat up. Stir fry for 1-2 minutes, stirring all the time
    so as not to catch it on the bottom.

4. Pour in the white wine and bring to the boil, stirring all the
    time. Turn the heat down and simmer for 3-4 minutes.

5. Pour in a quarter of the pre-heated stock and bring to a simmer,
    keep stirring. When the liquid is absorbed add another quarter
    of stock. Do this until all the stock has been absorbed. This will
    take about 20 minutes. At this stage the rice should be cooked.

6. Stir in the remaining butter, Parmesan cheese and coriander.
    Serve into bowls and top with the crème fraîche mixed with
    the lime.

7. Finally serve the risotto with a small dish of raita
    (see recipe below).

RAITA

PREPARATION TIME: 5 MINS

COOKING TIME: 1 MIN

INGREDIENTS

1 tsp cumin seeds

125g thick set natural curd or yoghurt

¼ tsp paprika

1 tbsp chopped coriander

1 tbsp chopped mint

INSTRUCTIONS

1. Heat a small pan over a low heat and dry roast the cumin seeds
    until they turn a darker shade. Allow the seeds to cool, and then
    crush them in a mortar and pestle.

2. Beat the curd or yoghurt until smooth. Stir in the cumin.

3. Put the raita into a serving dish.

4. Sprinkle the paprika, a few cumin seeds and herbs.

Beetroot contains potassium, magnesium, iron, vitamins A, B6 and C and folic acid. Research has also shown that regular beetroot intake can help to lower blood pressure.

SERVES 4

Roasted rib eye steak

BY SAM MOODY

PREPARATION TIME: 30 MINS

COOKING TIME: 30 MINS FOR THE SQUASH, 6 MINS FOR THE STEAK + 15 MINS RESTING TIME

INGREDIENTS

100g Le Puy lentils
200ml water
1 carrot
1 shallot
1 butternut squash, quartered
    lengthways
1 clove garlic
thyme
freshly ground black pepper and
    ground cumin, for seasoning
50ml olive oil
20g Xeres vinegar
4 good 10oz rib eye steak, well aged
rocket salad, for garnish

INSTRUCTIONS

1. Rinse the lentils, put 150ml of water in pan, add the lentils carrot and shallot. Bring to a simmer and cook over a medium heat until soft, topping up with water from time to time. Once cooked and cooled quickly, lentils will keep for up to 5 days in the fridge.

2. Line a tray with tinfoil and add the squash. Slice and add the garlic, pick and add the thyme. Season lightly with a little pepper and ground cumin, cover with 50ml olive oil and 50ml water, wrap tightly in foil and cook at 160°C for 30 minutes until the squash is soft.

3. Remove the squash from the foil, fork over to mash up and remove from the skins, add the vinegar and a couple of tablespoons of the lentils and their cooking liquid to make a ragout.

4. Allow the steak to come to room temperature and season lightly with pepper. Preheat a heavy based pan over a medium-high heat, sear on both side for 3 minutes each side, rest in a warm place for 15 minutes.

to serve:
Place the ragout on the base of the plate, slice the beef over the top, garnish with rocket salad.

Iron-deficiency anaemia is common after cancer treatment. Including lean red meat in your diet one or two times per week will significantly boost your iron intake.

SERVES 6

PREPARATION TIME: 5-10 MINS

COOKING TIME: 20-25 MINS

Roasted halibut steaks with summer ratatouille

BY GALTON BLACKISTON

INGREDIENTS

ratatouille:

2 red onions

1 large aubergine, the purple Italian
    variety is best

2 yellow peppers

2 red peppers

3 courgettes

1 small fennel bulb

275ml olive oil

1 clove of garlic, peeled and roughly
    chopped

freshly ground black pepper,
    for seasoning

450g baby vine tomatoes

25g basil, roughly chopped or torn

halibut:

25ml olive oil

25g butter

6 halibut steaks on the bone, each
weighing about 175g

ground black pepper, for seasoning

INSTRUCTIONS

ratatouille:

1. Preheat the oven to 220°C.

2. Peel the onions, cut into quarters and then cut each quarter
    lengthways again.

3. Roughly chop the remaining vegetables, and put into a large
    bowl with the onions.

4. Pour over the olive oil, add the garlic, and mix thoroughly with
    your hands. Spread out the vegetables in a roasting tin
    and season.

5. Place in the hot oven, and once the vegetables have started to
    colour, add the tomatoes and basil.

6. Mix well and return to the oven for a further 20 minutes or so,
    until the vegetables are well coloured, but are still reasonably
    crunchy in texture.

7. Check the seasoning and serve either hot or cold.

halibut:

1. Heat a non-stick frying pan, and then add the oil followed by
    the butter. Once it is foaming, fry the halibut steaks on each
    side until lightly golden (you may need to do this in batches to
    avoid overcrowding the pan).

2. Remove the steaks and place on a trivet in a roasting tin.
    Roast in the preheated oven for 8-10 minutes, until they are
    just cooked.

to serve:

Arrange some ratatouille neatly on each serving plate and place the
fish on top.

chef's tip:

Ask your fishmonger to cut the steaks from the middle of the fish,
preferably a large one weighing at least 4.5kg, so that they are of
equal thickness and will cook evenly. If you are using halibut off the
bone, it will need less cooking time.

The red and yellow capsicums in the ratatouille are an excellent source of beta-carotene, lycopene and fibre, as well as offering a host of antioxidants such as vitamin B6, folic acid and vitamins A, C and K. Try to include them in your diet frequently.

153

SERVES
4

PREPARATION TIME: 30 MINS

COOKING TIME: 1-1½ HRS

Juniper crusted loin of venison

BY SAM MOODY

INGREDIENTS

2-3 large Maris Piper
2 large carrots
2 turnip
1 parsnip
a little oil
500g trimmed venison loin
1 tsp Szechuan pepper
1 tsp juniper
small bunch parsley
1 clove garlic
1 handful dried bread crumbs
Dijon mustard
12 peeled chestnuts

INSTRUCTIONS

1. Peel all of the vegetables, chop into good sized even pieces and parboil.
2. Preheat a roasting tray with a little oil and starting with the potatoes, roast the vegetables until golden brown before everything else.
3. Lightly season the venison loin and then, in a hot pan with a little oil, sear all around golden brown on all sides, allow to rest
4. Toast the spice for a few minutes, then in a in a blender mix the parsley, garlic, spices and bread crumb together.
5. Brush the venison with Dijon mustard, top with the crumb; finish the venison in the oven for 5 minutes at 160°C.
6. Drop the chestnuts into your roasting vegetables, and cook for 5 minutes.
7. Carve the venison and assemble the vegetables on to a board. Serve.

Venison, like other red meats, is a good source of protein, iron and zinc. However, it has approximately 30% less fat and calories, making it a healthy alternative to beef or lamb.

SERVES 4

PREPARATION TIME: 10 MINS

COOKING TIME: 20 MINS

Grilled guinea fowl with pilaf rice

BY GALTON BLACKISTON

INGREDIENTS

drizzle rapeseed oil
4 breasts guinea fowl
60g butter
1 finely chopped shallot
100g basmati rice
200g chicken stock

INSTRUCTIONS

1. On a low heat place a large frying pan on the stove top, add a light drizzle of rapeseed oil. Add the guinea fowl to the pan skin side down (don't try to move the guinea breasts).

2. Slowly cook for about 10-15 minutes until the skin is crispy and the breasts are three quarters cooked. At this point turn your guinea fowl breasts over and place into the oven for 3-5 mins to finish off.

3. Remove from the oven and place the guinea fowl breasts on a cooling rack to rest before serving.

4. Preheat the oven to 170°C.

5. Heat a heavy bottomed pot on a medium heat, add 50g of butter and sweat off the shallots without colouring them.

6. Once cooked add the rice and chicken stock, place a cartouche on top, then put in the oven for 20 minutes or until the rice is cooked. Once cooked remove from the oven and add the rest of the butter. Season and serve hot.

to serve:
Place a big serving of the rice in the middle of the plate and place the guinea fowl breasts on top.

chef's tip:
Alternative ideas for serving – add roasted carrots, wild flowers, salad leaves or roasted tomatoes.

This recipe uses heart-healthy rapeseed oil which can withstand higher cooking temperatures better than olive oil. Try using rapeseed oil whenever you are cooking above 170 degrees, and reserve good quality olive-oil for adding flavour to cold dishes such as salads.

"This has a knock-on effect. When patients eat better and enjoy their food again, they feel better physically and emotionally: they become more active and engaged in other parts of their lives"

Dr Michelle Kohn

SERVES 2

PREPARATION TIME: 30 MINS
COOKING TIME: 35-40 MINS

Pot roasted breast of chicken and sauce bois boudran

BY MARK JORDAN

INGREDIENTS

1 whole chicken (about 1kg)
2 red peppers
2 green peppers
2 yellow peppers
1 leek
1 shallots
200ml tomato ketchup
1 pt water
50ml olive oil
50ml vinegar
fine beans

INSTRUCTIONS

1. Remove the legs and wings (use for another dish or freeze) from the chicken and place the chicken crown into boiling water for 20 minutes.
2. Whilst the chicken is cooking, dice the peppers, leek and the shallots and mix together. Add the ketchup along with the water, olive oil and vinegar, taste and season as required and leave at room temperature.
3. Remove the chicken from the boiling waters and allow to dry in its own heat. Place the whole crown into a pan and shallow fry in olive oil until golden brown all over. Remove and leave to rest for 5 minutes.

to serve:

1. Using a sharp knife, remove the breast of the chicken from the carcass.
2. Spoon over the sauce and drop the fine beans into a pan of boiling water to cook for 2 minutes. Arrange on top of the chicken and serve straight away.

Ketchup is a great source of the anti-inflammatory phytochemical, lycopene. Look out for artisan style tomato sauces that have a lower salt and sugar content than conventional ketchup, or trying making the salt-free spicy tomato dip on page 237.

SERVES
2

PREPARATION TIME: 20 MINS
COOKING TIME: 20 MINS

Grilled loin of rabbit with pearl barley and sweetcorn risotto

BY MARK JORDAN

INGREDIENTS

3 fresh rabbit loins
1 shallot
1 clove garlic
vegetable oil
250g pearl barley
600ml chicken stock
150ml crème fraîche
truffle
½ tin cooked sweetcorn and juice
50g shaved Parmesan
10 trumpet mushrooms

INSTRUCTIONS

1. Remove the fillets of the rabbit from the bone using a sharp knife and place in the fridge.
2. Meanwhile finely dice the shallots and the garlic and gently sauté with a little vegetable oil.
3. Add the pearl barley and stir bit by bit, adding a little of the chicken stock as the barley cooks. Add more of the stock until the barley is cooked and has a risotto texture. At this point put to one side and sauté the rabbit loins in a little vegetable oil until golden brown all over, this will take about 5-6 minutes.
4. Place the risotto back on the heat and add the crème fraîche, truffle, sweetcorn and juice and the grated Parmesan.

to serve:
Place a good spoonful of the risotto into the centre of a bowl and arrange the sauté rabbit loins all over the dish, in a separate pan sautéed the mushrooms and arrange all over the dish, serve straight away.

Pearl barley is a fibre-packed wholegrain that can benefit digestion and regulate bowel habits. It can be used as a nutritious alternative to risotto rice.

PREPARATION TIME: 30 MINS

COOKING TIME: 1 HR

Roast pigeon with walnuts and pomegranate

BY PETER FIORI

INGREDIENTS

4 squab pigeons, prepped for roasting (ask your butcher to do this)

pigeon glaze:
2 tbsp honey
2 tbsp pomegranate molasses
½ tsp black peppercorns, crushed
½ tsp green cardamom, crushed
4 tbsp extra virgin olive oil
2 tbsp boiling water

walnut sauce:
200g walnuts
3 tbsp extra virgin olive oil
1 white onion, fine dice
1 tsp ground cinnamon
½ tsp ground turmeric
1 tbsp tomato paste
1 tbsp honey
1 tbsp pomegranate molasses
1 bay leaf
400ml white chicken stock
juice ½ lemon
10g soft dark brown sugar

couscous:
100g couscous
1 tbsp extra virgin olive oil
150ml boiling water
1 lemon, juice and fine zest
¼ bunch coriander

garnish:
fresh pomegranate seeds
coriander micro-cress

INSTRUCTIONS

pigeon glaze:
Grind all the ingredients together in a pestle and mortar and set aside until needed.

walnut sauce:
1. Toast the walnuts at 180°C for 8-10 minutes until golden. Whilst still hot, rub between a tea towel to remove most of the skin. Cool and coarsely chop.
2. Sauté the onion on a medium heat with no colour until soft, add the spices, tomato paste and walnuts and cook for 4 minutes adding a little water if it begins to catch.
3. Finally add the rest of the ingredients and simmer very gently for about an hour until the mix is thick and rich.

couscous:
1. Place the couscous in a bowl and toss with the olive oil.
2. Pour over the boiling water, cling film and leave for 8-10 minutes.
3. Using a fork, gently fluff the grain and flavour with the lemon and coriander.

to serve:
1. Heat a heavy bottom frying pan with a little oil.
2. Brown the birds on each side for 2 minutes over a medium heat finishing on the back bone. Turn the heat to low and add the pigeon glaze to the pan, basting the birds for a further few minutes.
3. Place the pan in the oven at 180°C for about 4-5 minutes basting the pigeon glaze over regularly. This should give you a pink-medium doneness.
4. Take out from the pan and remove the legs by cutting around the natural seam with a sharp knife to expose the knuckle and then cutting through the ball and socket joint.

5. Place the legs back in the pan and cook for a further 5 minutes whilst the bird is resting.

6. Once rested, remove the breasts by cutting with the sharp point of a sharp knife along each side of the central breast plate and following down the bone gently pulling at the meat to expose the cutting point.

7. Serve the breasts and legs with the warmed walnut sauce, couscous, fresh pomegranate seeds and coriander micro-cress.

This rich, comforting Autumnal dish includes several cancer-fighting ingredients including pomegranate and walnuts, both of which contain ellagic acid, which in cell studies has been shown to have anti-cancer properties, particularly against prostate cancer.

Sea bream with tomato and corn salsa

BY JASON ATHERTON

SERVES
4

PREPARATION TIME: 20 MINS +
1 HR CHILLING TIME

COOKING TIME: 10 MINS

INGREDIENTS

salsa:
1 corn on the cob, kernels stripped
3 tomatoes, halved and deseeded
1 avocado, halved, peeled and stoned
½ cucumber, trimmed
½ yellow pepper, cored and deseeded
½ red onion, peeled
1 spring onion, trimmed
1 garlic clove, peeled
1 green chilli, halved and deseeded
juice of 1 lime
4 tbsp olive oil
2 tsp chopped coriander leaves

sea bream:
4 sea bream fillets (about 160g each),
    skin on
olive oil, brushing and drizzling
freshly ground black pepper,
    for seasoning
rocket leaves, to garnish

INSTRUCTIONS

salsa:
1. Simmer the corn kernels in a pan of boiling water until tender, about 6-8 minutes.
2. Drain, refresh under cold running water and drain well. Tip the corn kernels into a large bowl.
3. Dice the tomatoes, avocado, cucumber and yellow pepper; finely dice the red onion, spring onion, garlic and chilli. Add these ingredients to the corn with the lime juice, olive oil and coriander.
4. Toss to combine and season with pepper. Cover and chill for 1 hour.

sea bream:
1. Rinse the sea bream fillets, pat dry with kitchen paper and check for small bones, removing any with kitchen tweezers. Lightly score the skin side of the fish fillets, using a sharp knife. Cover and chill.
2. Brush the fish fillets with olive oil and season well. Heat a griddle pan or the grill to medium-high. When hot, add the fish, skin side down. Cook for 2-3 minutes on each side, depending on thickness, until just cooked through.

to serve:
Place a sea bream fillet on each warm plate, spoon on some of the chilled salsa, top with a pile of rocket and add a drizzle of olive oil.

This recipe uses raw garlic in the salsa. To get the greatest health benefits from garlic cloves, chop or crush them 10 minutes before needed in cooking and let them sit on the chopping board. This releases the sulphur containing phytonutrient allicin and increases our absorption of it.

Dashi is a type of stock, which becomes the base of many Japanese dishes. It requires a little extra effort to make your own dashi, rather than just buying it from a Japanese grocers, but it's worth taking the time to learn how to do this as you can use the same method to create a multitude of Japanese dishes. In this recipe, Peter Fiori has created a cancer-fighting concoction by combining chilli, ginger, onions, lemongrass, coriander and lime.

Steamed sea bass with hon dashi

BY PETER FIORI

SERVES
4

PREPARATION TIME: **1 HR**

COOKING TIME: **1 HR**

INGREDIENTS

4 x 140g sea bass per portion

hon dashi (stage 1):
1.1 litres water
½ red chilli, deseeded
30g fresh ginger
2 sticks lemon grass, bashed
3 kaffir lime leaves
zest 1 lime
½ bunch coriander stalks

hon dashi (stage 2, to finish):
2 tbsp soy sauce
juice ½ lime
5 spring onions, chopped
½ bunch coriander leaves

vegetable garnish:
1 long pimento red pepper
4 spring onions
4 baby courgettes
½ butternut squash, peeled

INSTRUCTIONS

hon dashi:
1. Bring to the boil all the ingredients in stage 1 and simmer gently for 5 minutes.
2. Remove from the heat and add the ingredients from stage 2.
3. Cling film and leave to cool until room temperature.
4. Pass through a fine sieve and chill until needed.

vegetable garnish:
Cut the vegetables into julienne of 2mm strips and keep until you are ready to serve.

to serve:
1. Place the hon dashi into a thick bottomed sauté pan and heat to just below simmering, approximately 80°C.
2. Place the bass into the dashi flesh side down. The liquid should come a third of the way up the fish.
3. Bring the liquid back up to heat and add the vegetables julienne.
4. Cover with a lid and cook in an oven at 180°C for about 4-5 minutes until the flesh of the fish has turned opaque and the vegetables have softened slightly.
5. Finish with some fresh coriander or micro coriander cress.

chef's tip:
This can also be enjoyed as a soup or broth with seafood, noodles, vegetables or other fresh ingredients.

CAULIFLOWER

Delicious when roasted

GARLIC

Flavoursome and adaptable seasoning

SERVES 2

PREPARATION TIME: 1 HR
COOKING TIME: 30 MINS

Paella of chicken, squid and prawns

BY JASON ATHERTON

INGREDIENTS

4 chicken thighs (bone in)
200g squid, cleaned
50g king prawns
4 tbsp olive oil
1 onion, peeled and diced
1 tsp paprika
pinch of saffron strands
1 tsp dried oregano
pinch of dried chilli flakes
1 tomato, diced
2 garlic cloves, peeled and finely
    chopped
250g paella rice
750ml fish stock
finely grated zest 1 orange
freshly ground pepper, for seasoning
3 tbsp vegetable oil
1 tbsp chopped parsley

INSTRUCTIONS

1. Preheat the oven to 150°C and put a baking tray in to heat up. Rinse the chicken thighs and trim off any fat.
2. Slice the squid pouches into 1cm rings, place in a bowl with the tentacles, cover and chill. Clean and peel the prawns.
3. Place a paella pan or shallow casserole dish over a medium heat and add 2 tablespoons of olive oil. Sweat off the onion, adding the paprika, saffron, oregano, chilli flakes, tomato and garlic.
4. Stir and cook for about 3-4 minutes until the onion and garlic are softened, then tip in the rice. Cook for about 3-4 minutes, stirring.
5. Pour in the fish stock and stir in the orange zest. Bring to the boil, stirring occasionally. Turn the heat down to a low simmer. Cook, uncovered, for about 15 minutes without stirring until the rice is tender, while retaining a bite.
6. While the paella is simmering, cook the chicken. Place a frying pan over a medium-high heat and add the vegetable oil. Pat the chicken thighs dry with kitchen paper and sear in the hot pan for 4-5 minutes on each side to colour and crisp the skin. Transfer to the hot baking tray and place in the oven for about 5 minutes to cook through.
7. To cook the squid, heat the remaining 2 tablespoons of olive oil in a large frying pan over a high heat. Fry the squid, in batches if necessary, for 1½-2 minutes until lightly coloured. Season with pepper.
8. Lightly fry off the prawns until pink in colour. This will take just a few minutes and can be done with the squid.
9. Just before serving toss two-thirds of the squid, prawns, and chopped parsley through the paella and check the seasoning. Top with the chicken thighs and scatter over the remaining parsley, prawns and squid.

to serve:
Serve the paella straight from the pan or divide between warm plates.

This is a great dish to share with friends and family. We have categorised it as an 'indulgent treat' because the skin is kept on the chicken thighs. Trimming the skin and excess fat from the chicken thighs would help to reduce the saturated fat and calorie count of the dish and mean it could be enjoyed more regularly.

SERVES 4

PREPARATION TIME: 1 HR

COOKING TIME: 2 HRS

Pulled mutton shepherd's pie

BY SIMON BOYLE

INGREDIENTS

2 tbsp olive oil

2kg shoulder of mutton

freshly ground black pepper,
   for seasoning

2 onions, peeled and finely chopped

2 sprigs fresh thyme

4 cloves garlic

25g butter

40g tomato purée

40g flour

300ml red wine

40ml Worcestershire sauce

1 litre chicken stock

freshly ground white pepper,
   for seasoning

750g mashed potato

100g cheddar cheese, grated

INSTRUCTIONS

1. In a large frying pan, heat the oil until hot, add the mutton, season with pepper and fry until well browned. Remove the meat from the pan and place in a roasting tray.

2. Add the onion to the pan with the thyme and garlic and a knob of butter and cook until soft and translucent. Add the meat and tomato purée, and then sprinkle over the flour. Cook stirring constantly for 2-3 minutes to cook the flour.

3. Add the red wine and Worcestershire sauce. Add the chicken stock, bring back to a simmer and add all of this into the roasting pan with the mutton.

4. Braise this for at least 2 hours at 150°C, maybe longer, until the meat is flaking from the bone. At this point, remove from the liquid and cool so that it can be handled. Should the stock require further thickening, reduce on the heat as required.

5. Flake the meat and add enough gravy to moisten well, warm the remaining gravy later to serve at the table. Reserve the bone and trimmings for a lovely pot of Scotch Broth if desired.

6. Spoon the meat and gravy into a suitable pie dish. Spread out and level off the meat and sauce. Chill for an hour if time allows.

7. Using a piping bag or spoon cover the meat with buttery mash. Sprinkle with cheddar cheese.

8. Bake at 190°C for 25-35 minutes until golden brown, serve immediately.

This nutritious alternative to a traditional Shepherd's Pie uses lycopene-rich tomato purée, resveratrol-rich red wine and the allium vegetables, onions and garlic, to add extra flavour to the meat filling.

Halibut with a tomato and lemon verbena relish

BY PETER FIORI

SERVES
4

PREPARATION TIME: 20 MINS

COOKING TIME: 10 MINS

INGREDIENTS

4 x 150g halibut portions
freshly ground black pepper,
    for seasoning
extra virgin olive oil, to brush

tomato relish:
16 cherry vine tomatoes
½ cucumber, ½cm dice
1 apple, ½cm dice
2 tbsp fine capers
200ml extra virgin olive oil
12 lemon segments, ½cm dice
16 brown anchovy fillets, diced
2 tbsp basil, ½cm dice
1 tbsp lemon verbena, ½cm dice

INSTRUCTIONS

1. Boil the kettle.
2. Season the halibut with a little pepper, brush a thick bottomed frying pan with a little olive oil and place the fish in.
3. Pour the boiling water a third of the way up the side of the fish and place a lid on top.
4. Place this into the oven at 180°C for 6-8 minutes until the fish is opaque, it should be about 50°C. You can also test this by pushing a meat skewer through the side of the fish and leaving for 5 seconds, it will be warm to the touch if cooked, but not hot!

tomato relish:

1. Quarter the cherry vine tomatoes and place in a pan with the diced cucumber, apple, capers, oil, lemon dice and anchovies.
2. When serving, warm to blood temperature and finish with the basil and lemon verbena, spoon over the fish and garnish with some fresh sprigs of lemon verbena.

This omega-3 rich dish is flavoured with lemon verbena. The leaves and the flowering tops of the verbena plant have been used for medicinal purposes for centuries. Verbena has been reported to aid digestion, help with sleep disorders and have antibacterial properties. You could also try making a lemon verbena tea by seeping the flowers and leaves in boiling water.

SERVES
1

PREPARATION TIME: 40 MINS

COOKING TIME: 20 MINS

Grilled tuna salad, tomatoes, olives and basil

BY JOHN WILLIAMS

INGREDIENTS

6 cherry tomatoes

6 Niçoise olives

1 shallots

6 mint leaves

6 basil leaves

6 coriander leaves

3 mache bouquet

20g cucumber

1/3 avocado

35ml extra virgin olive oil

15ml Cabernet Sauvignon vinegar

150g tuna steak

INSTRUCTIONS

1. Cut the cherry tomatoes in half and remove the stones from the olives.
2. Dice the shallots.
3. Pick the leaves from the mint, basil and coriander.
4. Separate the leaves of the mache and wash
5. Dice and peel the cucumber, cut long ways twice then remove the seeds and cut into large dice.
6. Peel and large slice the avocado.
7. Prepare the dressing of oil and vinegar and gently combine with all of the salad ingredients.
8. Finally, blend the herb leaves through the salad leaving them whole.

to serve:

1. Heat a griddle pan until hot, brush the tuna steak with olive oil and a little seasoning, place on to a hot griddle for 30-40 seconds each side then remove.
2. Place the mixed salad on the plate and dress the tuna steak.

This recipe is perfect for people looking after their hearts as it uses three good sources of heart-healthy fats; avocado, olive oil and tuna. If you can't find Cabernet Sauvignon vinegar, any white wine vinegar will enhance the flavour of this dish.

Farm rabbit casserole with garlic and lemon

BY DANIEL GALMICHE

SERVES 4

PREPARATION TIME: 20 MINS

COOKING TIME: 45-50 MINS

INGREDIENTS

1 lemon, grated and juiced
2kg farm rabbit, cut into 8 pieces
4 tbsp olive oil
freshly ground black pepper,
    for seasoning
knob of butter
4 garlic cloves, unpeeled, crushed
500ml chicken stock
2 sprigs fresh thyme or basil

INSTRUCTIONS

1. Preheat the oven to 200°C.
2. Place the zest and juice of the lemon in a large bowl, then add the rabbit pieces, a glug of olive oil and season with freshly ground black pepper. Leave to marinate for 5 minutes.
3. Warm a heatproof casserole dish on a medium heat and add the butter, the remaining olive oil and the rabbit and sauté until golden brown. You may have to do this in two sections depending on the size of your pan. Put the garlic cloves and lemon marinade into the pan and deglaze – there will be a bit of a splash and some smoke, allow it to evaporate for a few minutes and then add the stock and the herbs. Bring to the boil briefly then place in the oven for 30-35 minutes.
4. When cooked, remove the rabbit from the casserole to a serving dish and keep warm in the oven.
5. Return the casserole dish to the heat, bring the remaining liquid to the boil, then reduce and simmer until it has the consistency of a light syrup. Pour over the rabbit and serve with buttered spinach.

This delicious, wintry one-pot casserole is simple but full of flavour. When served with the wilted spinach is an excellent source of lean protein and iron.

PREPARATION TIME: 15 MINS

COOKING TIME: 1 HR FOR THE
TOMATO STEW, EGGS 10 MINS

Baked eggs with tomato, onions and sweet peppers

BY ANDREW FAIRLIE

INGREDIENTS

100ml light olive oil
2 large onions sliced
2 red peppers, thinly sliced
2 yellow peppers, thinly sliced
1 tsp Muscovado sugar
1 tsp chopped thyme leaves
1 small red chilli, thinly sliced
large pinch ground toasted
    cumin seeds
1 bay leaf
6 ripe tomatoes, roughly chopped
freshly ground black pepper,
    for seasoning
8 free range eggs

INSTRUCTIONS

1. In a large flat saucepan heat the oil. Add the onions and sauté until they start to colour.

2. Add the peppers, sugar, thyme, red chilli, cumin seeds and bay leaf. Continue to cook on high heat till they start to colour.

3. Add the chopped tomatoes and continue to cook over a medium heat for 15 minutes, stirring occasionally.

4. Cook until you have a thick sauce consistency. This part of the dish can be prepared up to two days in advance, it's a very handy base to have in a sealed container in the fridge.

5. Divide the mixture between individual frying pans, put onto a medium heat to warm up. Make two gaps in the pepper mix in each pan and carefully break an egg into each gap. Sprinkle with freshly ground pepper, cover the pans with a lid and cook gently in a low oven for 10 minutes until the eggs are just set.

6. Serve immediately with some sourdough toast.

This recipe is a variation of shakshuka, a traditional Israeli dish of baked eggs. The vitamin C, from the tomatoes and sweet peppers, aids the absorption of the iron from the eggs. You can get the same effect by pairing roasted tomatoes with your steak or a fresh orange with your fortified breakfast cereals.

PREPARATION TIME: 30 MINS

COOKING TIME: 30 MINS,
SAUCE 30 MINS

Poached chicken with aromatic bouillon

BY JOHN WILLIAMS

INGREDIENTS

1 chicken crown with double breast
   on the carcass
1 onion
2 celery sticks
1 carrot
¼ leek
1 star anise
1 bouquet garni
5 litres chicken stock
6 mushrooms
1 bay leaf
bunch of tarragon

to garnish:
baby turnips
baby carrots
radish
asparagus
truffle
celeriac purée

INSTRUCTIONS

1. Place the chicken into a large pan and cover with just enough chicken stock or water.
2. Place the onion, celery, carrot, leek, star anise and bouquet garni into the same pan, bring to the boil and very gently simmer for approximately 25 minutes.
3. Remove the skin and gently simmer the stock with the mushrooms and any bones from the chicken. Reduce by 50%.
4. Pass through a sieve and finish with the bay and tarragon leaves to give an aromatic flavour to the bouillon.
5. Blanch the garnish items (minus the truffle and celeriac purée) in water until tender and refresh on service.
6. Remove the breast from the carcass and place onto a hot plate and dress with the celeriac purée, vegetables and the truffle. Pour the bouillon over the chicken. Serve immediately.

chef's tip:
It is better to cook the breast on the carcass as this gives more flavour, the skin can then be removed.

This light refreshing dish is particularly suited to people who may be experiencing taste changes or a dry mouth after cancer treatment as the bouillon uses a combination of vegetables, herbs and spices to add flavour and moisture to the chicken breast.

PREPARATION TIME: 25-30 MINS

COOKING TIME: 20 MINS

Sea bream baked in sea salt, fennel salad with orange and lime

BY DANIEL GALMICHE

INGREDIENTS

sea bream:

2 egg whites

½ lime, zest and juice

zest ½ orange or grapefruit

1.8kg rock sea salt

4 x fillets sustainable, farmed
    sea bream

8 small greaseproof paper sheets,
    cut in rectangle the size of the fillet

salad:

1 orange, small, zest + segments
    (can also be a small pink grapefruit)

1 small fennel bulb

2 tbsp of olive oil

½ tbsp reduced balsamic vinegar.

½ small handful of roughly chopped
    chives

2 sprig of chervil

See page 256 for stage-by-stage
photos to illustrate cooking the fish.

INSTRUCTIONS

sea bream:

1. Preheat the oven to 190°C.
2. Place the egg whites into a large mixing bowl and whisk until stiff peaks form when the whisk is removed from the bowl.
3. Grate in the lime and grapefruit zest. Add the sea salt and mix by hand.
4. Line a baking tray with a layer of the salt mixture a touch bigger then that of the 4 fillets. Place 4 rectangle sheets of greaseproof paper onto it, then a fillet onto each of the paper, skin up, then another sheet of greaseproof on the top, and cover completely with the remaining salt mix, pressing it down firmly around the fish. This way, the fish will not be salty, but only take on a very delicate flavour. Note, use a tray large enough so you can bake the 4 fillets together.
5. Bake in the oven for 12-14 minutes, then remove from the oven and leave to rest for 2 minutes without touching the salt crust.
6. During the resting time, finish the salad, then break the salt crust and discard. Lift the paper one piece at the time, so that the fish stays warm. Lift the skin from one side of the fish to the other as shown in the images and serve hot.

fennel salad:

1. Grate the zest of the orange/grapefruit and set aside.
2. Peel and cut into segments from between the membrane, do this over a bowl so you can collect the juice you will need for the dressing.
3. Take the outer part of the fennel, wash, cut in half length ways and using a mandoline, cut it very fine. Note; beware of the blade and use the guard.
4. Just before serving, when the fish is on the plate, mix together in a bowl half of the juice, olive oil and balsamic vinegar, then throw in the fennel, herbs and segments. Mix together and serve immediately while the fennel is still crunchy, as it is important to get the freshness of the salad.

chef's tip:

You can use a small pink grapefruit instead of the orange.

In this recipe greaseproof paper is used to ensure the fish fillet
does not directly touch the sea-salt crust.

PREPARATION TIME: 20 MINS

COOKING TIME: 15 MINS

Fillet of cod with coriander, tomato and garlic 'en papillotte'

BY DANIEL GALMICHE

INGREDIENTS

4 x 150g portions of cod

4 cloves of garlic, skin on, crushed

4 tbsp olive oil

2 large tomatoes, sliced

small bunch of coriander leaves, chopped, no stalks

freshly ground black pepper, for seasoning

INSTRUCTIONS

1. Get your fishmonger to skin, pin-bone and fillet your fish.

2. Preheat the oven to 200°C and bring a small pan of water to the boil.

3. Pat the fish dry on kitchen towel. Season and leave while preparing the rest of the dish.

4. Blanch the garlic in its skin for 2 minutes, refresh in cold water and pat dry, that way it will be cooked at the same time as the fish when it's en papillotte.

5. Place 4 rectangular sheets of aluminium foil 45x25cm, shiny side down onto the worktop and drizzle half the olive oil on each. You need to put all the ingredients on one side of the foil so that you will be able to fold it in half like a piece of paper after you have laid all the ingredients inside.

6. Put a few slices of tomato and half the coriander leaves in each and season with freshly ground black pepper.

7. Lay the cod on top of the tomatoes, then add the garlic, the rest of the coriander and another drizzle of olive oil.

8. Fold the aluminium over the fish then fold over along the edges to seal securely. Make sure it is well sealed so that none of the the liquid is released and place in the oven on a tray and cook for 15 minutes.

9. Remove and rest in foil without opening for a further 2 minutes. Now comes the rush of aromas – open each parcel being careful not to lose any of the juice inside and serve with coriander scented rice.

chef's tip:

You can make this dish with so many combinations: ginger, lemongrass, chilli and coriander, or lemon and basil, or lime and parsley – experiment – you won't be disappointed.

Steaming fish in foil or baking paper is a great way to retain its
moisture without needing to add too much oil.

SERVES 4

PREPARATION TIME: 15 MINS

COOKING TIME: 60-80 MINS

Grilled marinated chicken in sumac, sweet potato gratin

BY ANDREW FAIRLIE

INGREDIENTS

3 tbs Greek yoghurt
2 tsp ground sumac
2 tbs lemon juice
2 cloves garlic, crushed
8 organic chicken thighs

sweet potato gratin:
6 medium sweet potatoes
6 garlic cloves, crushed
5 tbs roughly chopped sage
1 tbsp olive oil
250ml low fat whipping cream

INSTRUCTIONS

chicken:

1. In a bowl, whisk together the yoghurt, sumac, juice and garlic. Add the meat to the bowl and massage the marinade into the meat. Transfer the meat into a clean plastic tray, cover with cling film and place in the fridge overnight.
2. The next day, heat the oven to 220°C. Lay the chicken pieces onto a large baking tray and place into the hot oven. After 5 minutes, lower the temperature to 180°C and continue to cook for another 15 minutes until chicken is just about cooked.
3. Place the chicken under a hot grill for another 3 or 4 minutes to give it extra colour and finish cooking it through.

sweet potato gratin:

1. Preheat the oven to 200°C.
2. Wash the potatoes but do not peel them, cut them into 3mm slices with a mandoline.
3. In a bowl mix the potato, garlic, sage and oil.
4. Arrange the slices into an ovenproof dish placing them in one by one so as they are arranged neatly and snugly to cover the baking dish.
5. Cover the dish with tin foil and roast in the hot oven for 35 to 40 minutes, remove the tin foil, pour over the cream and return to the oven uncovered for another 40 minutes. Test the potatoes are cooked by inserting the tip of a sharp knife at various points, the potatoes should be soft.
6. Can be served straight from the oven or at room temperature.

Sumac is a spice made from the dried, ground fruits of a flowering shrub. Sumac has a tart flavour that is delicious when sprinkled on fish, chicken, hummus or rice dishes. It makes a useful addition to the kitchen spice rack.

SERVES 4

PREPARATION TIME: 40 MINS

COOKING TIME: 3 HRS

Braised lamb neck tagine, quinoa and sweet potato

BY PETER FIORI

INGREDIENTS

lamb neck tagine:
2 tsp ras el hanout
1 tsp cumin seeds
1 tsp black peppercorns
1 tsp ground cinnamon
2 tsp lemon coriander seed
2 tsp ground coriander
1 tsp ground ginger
4 lamb necks trimmed of excess fat
1 shallot, finely chopped
4 cloves garlic, paste
30g ginger, finely chopped
½ red chilli, finely chopped
2 pinches saffron
1 tbsp tomato paste
2 tbsp honey
50ml Pedro Ximenez balsamic
150g golden raisins
250g dates, stoned and 1cm dice
150g dried apricots, 1cm dice
4 tomatoes, 1cm dice
500ml white chicken stock
300ml lamb jus
¼ bunch coriander, all shredded
50g flaked almonds, toasted

quinoa:
150g quinoa
1 peeled sweet potato, 1cm dice
1 sweet corn cob
1 red chilli deseeded, finely diced
1 green chilli deseeded, finely diced
50g pumpkin seeds, toasted
30g sunflower seeds, toasted
1 orange, segments 1cm diced
¼ bunch coriander leaves, shredded
juice and zest ½ lemon
3 dsp extra virgin olive oil
freshly ground black pepper

INSTRUCTIONS

1. Place the ras el hanout, cumin seeds, black peppercorns, ground cinnamon, lemon coriander seed, ground coriander and ground ginger in a pestle and mortar or spice grinder and grind to a coarse powder.
2. Heat a frying pan to a medium-high heat, season and brown the lamb necks and set aside.
3. In a braising, heavy bottomed pan, sauté in oil the shallot, garlic, 30g chopped ginger and chilli until softened. Then add the spices and saffron and gently cook for 2-3 minutes adding water if too dry.
4. Next add the tomato paste and cook for 2 minutes, then add the honey and vinegar and reduce until a syrup.
5. Now add the fruit including the tomatoes, the stock and jus and bring to the boil. Place in the lamb necks and cover with a greaseproof paper cartouche and a lid. Put in the oven and cook at 140°C for approximately 3 hours or until it is soft enough to cut with a spoon.
6. To finish, stir through the coriander and top with toasted almonds.

quinoa:
1. Bring a large pan of salted water to the boil and simmer the quinoa for 10-12 minutes until soft. Drain in a sieve.
2. Sauté the sweet potato in olive oil until softened.
3. Cook the corn for 5 minutes in boiling water, then on a char-grill, griddle until blackened.
4. With a sharp knife set the corn kernels free and mix everything in a bowl to create the warm quinoa salad.

to serve:
Remove the lamb from the sauce and slice thickly, about 2cm thick, and serve with the warm quinoa salad.

Although the ingredients list for this Moroccan-inspired dish is extensive, the one-pot cooking method is simple. This is perfect for a Sunday dinner to share with family and friends.

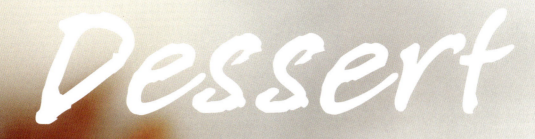

Dessert

Although, it is not recommended to have a pudding or dessert every day, the nutrient-dense recipes in this section have all been developed to ensure that they contain cancer-protective ingredients such as strawberries, dark chocolate, tofu, ginger, green tea and almonds.

If you, or your loved one, have lost weight during your cancer treatment, these recipes can be used to supplement a healthy balanced diet and promote weight gain.

If you are looking to lose weight or maintain a healthy body weight, use these dishes less frequently and try to choose those which have not been categorised as an indulgent treat.

195

PREPARATION TIME: 5 MINS

COOKING TIME: 10 MINS

INGREDIENTS

400g water
400g caster sugar
1 old vanilla pod
250g fresh strawberries
1 ripe mango

Poached strawberries with mango sorbet

BY GALTON BLACKISTON

INSTRUCTIONS

1. Place the water, sugar and vanilla pod into a saucepan and put on a high heat. Bring to the boil, remove from the heat and allow to cool.

2. Once cold, take 300g of the sugar and water mix, and place in a saucepan with the strawberries, place on a medium heat and bring to a simmer. Cover with cling film and allow to cool for 5-10 minutes, this will just poach the strawberries nicely without having to worry about them.

3. Peel the mango using a potato peeler and remove as much meat as possible.

4. Place into a blender with the remainder of the sugar and water, blend until a smooth purée and pass through a sieve if needed.

5. Churn in an ice cream machine according to manufacturer's instructions or place into a container and freeze, stirring every now and then until a sorbet consistency is achieved; about 2-3 hours will be enough.

to serve:
Place some strawberries into the bottom of a bowl with a little of the cooking liquid and scoop a large scoop of the mango sorbet on top with a little garden mint if you have some.

SERVES
2-3

PREPARATION TIME: 10 MINS

Chocolate dipped strawberries

BY MARK JORDAN

INGREDIENTS

1 punnet strawberries
1lb good quality chocolate
50g chopped nuts

INSTRUCTIONS

1. Melt the chocolate in the microwave, stirring as it melts. Be careful not to burn the chocolate.
2. Skewer the strawberries with a cocktail stick and dip into the chocolate, allowing the excess chocolate to fall off.
3. Whilst the chocolate is still melted, sprinkle some of the nuts over the top.
4. Place in a cool place and allow the chocolate to set.

PREPARATION TIME: 30 MINS

COOKING TIME: 10 MINS

Blueberry and elderflower sorbet with buckwheat and rosehip pancake cornets

BY SIMON BOYLE

INGREDIENTS

sorbet;
250g granulated sugar, or caster sugar
300ml water
½ unwaxed lemon
5 heads elderflower
2 punnets blueberries
1 punnet blueberries, for garnish

pancakes:
275ml flora pro-active milk
1 egg
1 tsp butter, melted
50g buckwheat flour
50g plain white flour
(gluten free is fine)
3 rosehip tea bags

to finish:
1 punnet blueberries, for garnish
100g Greek yoghurt

INSTRUCTIONS

sorbet:

1. Put the sugar into a pan with the water and bring up to the boil, stirring until the sugar has completely dissolved.

2. While the sugar syrup is heating, finely grate the zest of the lemon into a large glass jug. Squeeze the juice of the lemon, and add to the zest.

3. Shake the elderflowers outside, to make sure there are no insects hanging on for dear life, and then place in the jug also.

4. Pour over the boiling syrup. Cover with cling film and then leave until it reaches room temperature. The longer you leave it the more it will infuse. I usually do this over night, but you really don't need to.

5. Return the syrup back to the boil and strain into a liquidiser. Add the blueberries and blitz until smooth. Strain once again pushing as much juice out as possible, leave to get to room temperature.

6. Place into an ice cream machine and churn according to manufacturer's instructions.

7. Once frozen, transfer from the machine into a plastic dish with a sealable lid and place into the freezer until needed. This sorbet can keep for a few months but I bet it won't!

pancake cornets:

1. Put the milk, egg, and melted butter into a liquidiser and blend thoroughly for 15-30 seconds.

2. Then add the flours and liquidise again for 15-30 seconds.

3. Open the tea bags and sprinkle in the rosehip tea; stir in. If possible, let the batter stand to allow the mixture to settle before cooking. If it becomes too thick, just let it down with a little milk.

4. Heat a very flat non-stick pan until very hot; add a touch of butter or your favourite spread and a small ladle of pancake mix. Sway the pan around to ensure the pancake mix is equally spread around. After 20-30 seconds, using a palette knife, turn the pancake over. (Do not colour too much, as the tea is quite nice to look at). After 4-5 seconds turn onto a plate and start the next.

5. Cut a line from the centre of each crepe and fold to form a small cornet and place in a lightly greased shot glass or something similar in shape or size, making sure the edges are folded over.

6. Place in a medium oven for approximately 3-4 minutes. Take out and let them cool down before serving. The cornets can be pre-prepared and stored in an old ice cream box.

7. Serve the pancake cornets with a big spoon of sorbet, a sprinkling of blueberries and a big dollop of lightly sweetened Greek yoghurt. Finish with a pinch of rosehip tea leaves.

Note:

If this all seems too much trouble or elderflower is out of season, you can buy wonderful elder flower cordial. Bring 375ml of it to the boil before adding the blueberries – it helps to purée them down and bring their flavour out.

SERVES 4

PREPARATION TIME: 30 MINS

COOKING TIME: 10 MINS

Almond panna cotta, apricots and sorbet

BY MARK JORDAN

INGREDIENTS

panna cotta:
300g sliced almonds
400ml double cream
200ml milk
3 leaves gelatine
100g caster sugar

sorbet:
300ml apricot purée
300ml stock syrup

apricot:
1 pt water
1 tea bag
1 lemon
200g sugar
1 orange
½kg of dried apricot

INSTRUCTIONS

panna cotta:
1. Toast the almonds until golden and then add to the double cream and milk, bring this to the boil and leave to marinate for 30 minutes.
2. Melt the gelatine in cold water and then add to the milk mix. Pass this through a fine sieve and add the sugar.
3. Pour the liquid into 4 glass bowls and refrigerate.

sorbet:
1. Boil the purée and stock syrup together and then place into the fridge to cool.
2. Pour the mix into a sorbet machine and churn according to manufacturer's instructions until frozen. Store in the freezer until required.

apricots:
Place all the ingredients together in a saucepan and slowly bring up to a simmer. Remove from the heat and allow the mix to cool completely.

to serve:
Once the panna cotta has set, arrange some apricots on top of it and finish with a spoonful of sorbet.

PREPARATION TIME: 24 HRS IN
ADVANCE FOR SPICED PINEAPPLE,
1 HR FOR THE CANDIED GINGER

COOKING TIME: 10 MINS

Spiced pineapple with coconut sorbet and candied ginger

BY JASON ATHERTON

INGREDIENTS

spiced pineapple:
½ pineapple (cut lengthways)
250g granulated or caster sugar
1 vanilla pod
10g fresh root ginger, peeled
    and chopped
1 lemongrass stalk, trimmed and cut
    into 2 cm pieces
2g cloves
5g black peppercorns
5 star anise pods

candied ginger:
12g fresh root ginger, peeled
200g caster sugar, plus more
    for coating

to serve:
4 scoops of coconut sorbet
small handful of tiny coriander leaves

INSTRUCTIONS

spiced pineapple:
1. Trim and peel the pineapple half. Cut it lengthways in half again and remove the core. Now slice the pineapple in half crossways. Using a sharp knife, slice the halves thinly lengthways into 5mm thick slices. You need 20-24 slices.
2. Melt the sugar in a very large heavy-based pan over a medium heat, stirring gently to ensure it melts evenly. Increase the heat slightly and cook until the melted sugar forms a dark caramel.
3. Reduce the heat to medium low and add the vanilla pod, ginger, lemongrass and spices. Stir over the heat for about 1 minute. Now stir in 75ml water, taking care as the hot caramel will splutter.
4. Lay the pineapple slices in the spiced caramel and cook, flipping the sides over often for 3-4 minutes until softened, but retaining their shape. Remove from the heat.
5. Carefully transfer the pineapple slices to a large dish, making sure they are completely submerged in the caramel. Leave to stand for 24 hours at room temperature.

candied ginger:
1. Finely slice the root ginger, on a mandoline if possible. Bring a small pan of water to the boil and blanch the ginger slices for 1-2 minutes, then drain. Repeat this process 3 times, changing the water each time, to mellow the sharp spiciness.
2. Place the sugar in a saucepan with 200ml water and slowly bring to the boil, stirring to dissolve the sugar. Add the blanched ginger and allow to simmer over a medium-low heat for 4-5 minutes. Remove with a slotted spoon and drain on a wire rack. Cool slightly, then toss in a little caster sugar to coat. Leave to dry at room temperature for an hour or until crisp.

to serve:
Using a slotted spoon, arrange 5 or 6 pineapple slices on each plate and drizzle with the spiced caramel sauce. Top with a scoop of coconut sorbet and decorate with candied ginger and coriander leaves.

PREPARATION TIME: 30 MINS + 2 HRS
MACERATING TIME

COOKING TIME: 30 MINS

Cherries in sweet wine, star anise ice cream

BY PETER FIORI

INGREDIENTS

cherries in sweet wine:
500g cherries
375ml dessert wine
50g caster sugar
1 vanilla pod, split
1 tbsp grenadine
4 tsp arrowroot
2 tsp water

star anise ice cream:
6 egg yolks (small eggs)
130g honey
500ml skimmed milk
½ vanilla pod, split
4 star anise

INSTRUCTIONS

cherries in sweet wine:

1. Stone the cherries carefully, put the stones in a plastic bag and crush them coarsely with the bottom of a heavy pan. Place the seeds in a pan with the sweet wine, sugar, vanilla pod and grenadine.
2. Bring the mixture to the boil. Dilute the arrowroot in water and whisk into the mixture. Stir until thickened.
3. Strain the syrup through a sieve over the pitted cherries, place all back into the pan and bring to boil. Simmer for 4 minutes, cover and set aside to macerate for 2 hours, then place in the fridge.

star anise ice cream:

1. Mix the egg yolks with the honey in a bowl.
2. Boil the skimmed milk with the vanilla and crushed star anise. Cover and infuse for 15 minutes.
3. Reheat the milk and pour this over the egg yolk and honey mixture whisking all the time.
4. Put the mix in a pan and heat until the mix coats the back of a spoon (85°C), pass through a sieve, cool and churn in an ice cream maker according to manufacturer's instructions.

to serve:
Spoon the cherries into individual bowls and top with a scoop of the ice cream.

SERVES 4

PREPARATION TIME: 30 MINS

COOKING TIME: 10 MINS

INGREDIENTS

grapefruit salsa:

2 pink grapefruits, medium sized

200g unrefined caster sugar

4 flower heads of lavender
(fresh or dried)

chocolate pot:

250ml double cream

½ vanilla pod, cut in half and
seeds scraped out

75g dark organic chocolate, at least
70% or higher

2 large egg yolks

100g unrefined caster sugar

50g unsalted butter

Chocolate pot with pink grapefruit and lavender salsa

BY SIMON BOYLE

INSTRUCTIONS

grapefruit salsa:

1. Peel the zest from 1 pink grapefruit; remove any white pith from the peelings. Cut into very fine shreds.
2. Cut the outer pith from both the grapefruits, cutting right down to the flesh with a sharp knife. Segment and dice the grapefruit, saving the juices that are squeezed out and discarding any pips that you happen to come across.
3. Put the sugar into a pan (use one with a metallic or white interior, not black, so that you can see the colour of the sugar clearly as it caramelises) with 100ml water and the grapefruit rind shreds.
4. Stir over a moderate heat until the sugar has completely dissolved. Bring up to the boil and stop stirring. Boil hard, swirling the pan occasionally to even out hot spots, but never stirring, until the sugar darkens to a hazelnut-brown caramel. Take off the heat and sit until it cools for 2-3 minutes.
5. Now at arm's length, pour in the diced grapefruit, juice and lavender.
6. Swirl the pan, and leave to cool, the lavender flavour will start to come through.

chocolate pot:

1. In a thick-bottomed pot, heat the cream, vanilla seeds and pod until near boiling. Remove from the heat and set aside for 1 minute. Take out the vanilla pod before adding the chocolate.
2. Stir in the chocolate until melted and smooth. Reserve for two minutes to cool.
3. In a separate bowl, whisk together the egg yolks and sugar. Whisk into the chocolate cream.
4. Add the butter and stir until smooth and shiny. Pour into individual serving pots.

to serve:

Serve the chocolate pot, slightly chilled with a dollop of lightly whipped cream. The salsa should be at room temperature or lightly chilled in a shot glass to pour over the chocolate pot before eating.

chef's tip:

If you add the butter when the chocolate isn't cool enough it will make the chocolate look as if it has split. To rectify this allow the mixture to cool a little longer before stirring in some cold milk, a little at a time, until you have a smooth consistency again.
If you don't like grapefruit you can swap for oranges.

PREPARATION TIME: 20 MINS,
+ 30 MINS RESTING

COOKING TIME: 8 MINS

Gluten-free chocolate and ginger fondant
BY DANIEL GALMICHE

INGREDIENTS

A little cocoa powder; 70% cocoa
    solids, for dusting
100g dark chocolate, 70% cocoa solids
100g unsalted butter, plus extra
    for greasing
3 eggs
4 tbsp caster sugar
4 tbsp corn flour
1 ball stem ginger, finely chopped

garnish:
100g fresh raspberries
1 tbsp caster sugar
zest ½ lime
1 tbsp balsamic vinegar

INSTRUCTIONS

1. Butter 4 small ramekins or pudding moulds and dust with
   cocoa powder.
2. Put the chocolate and butter in a heatproof bowl and rest it over
   a pan of gently simmering water making sure that the bottom
   of the bowl does not touch the water, Heat, stirring occasionally,
   until the chocolate has melted. Alternatively, melt very gently
   in short bursts in the microwave, stirring regularly until melted.
   Remove from the heat.
3. Whisk together the eggs and sugar with a mixer or electric
   whisk for at least 15 minutes until they are almost white in
   colour, very shiny and nearly at soft peak stage. This will give a
   really light, crusty outside to the fondant, but the inside will be
   melting soft.
4. Pour the melted chocolate and butter into the mix and whisk to
   combine. Sift the cornflour over the top and fold in, then fold in
   the stem ginger taking care not to over mix at the point.
5. Divide the mixture among the prepared ramekins, filling
   three-quarters full. Put on a baking tray in a cool place to rest
   for 30 minutes.

garnish:
1. Put all the ingredients into a bowl, cover with cling film and
   shake very gently by swirling around.
2. Set aside to marinate for 20 minutes.

to serve:
1. Preheat the oven to 220°C. Bake the fondants for 5-6 minutes
   until the fondant has risen above the moulds and has formed a
   light crust on top and around the edges.
2. Remove and turn out straight onto a serving plate, spoon some
   of the raspberries to the side of the fondant; this is so refreshing
   it will cut through the richness of the chocolate.

SERVES 4

PREPARATION TIME: 30 MINS + 2 HRS
MACERATING TIME

COOKING TIME: 1 HR

INGREDIENTS

tapioca pudding:
125g tapioca
450ml coconut milk
1 kaffir lime leaf
10g peeled root ginger, grated
½ vanilla pod split
3 tbsp palm sugar

red fruit sorbet:
100g blackberries
200g raspberries
125g redcurrants
125g blackcurrants
100g honey

Coconut and ginger tapioca pudding with red fruit sorbet

BY PETER FIORI

INSTRUCTIONS

tapioca pudding:
1. Place the tapioca in a pan and cover with cold water and soak for 30 minutes.
2. In a separate pan, bring to the boil the 450 ml of coconut milk, kaffir lime leaf, grated ginger, vanilla and 3 tablespoons of palm sugar. Remove from the heat and leave to infuse for 30 minutes. Strain into a bowl.
3. Place the tapioca over a medium heat and simmer for 20-25 minutes until it turns transparent. Note, make sure that you have at least 8 times the amount of water to tapioca.
4. Strain into a sieve and rinse under cold running water for 30 seconds.
5. Mix the strained tapioca with the coconut milk mixture, pour into your serving glasses, leave in the fridge overnight to mature in flavour.

red fruit sorbet:
Take all the berries and honey and put in a warm place to macerate for 2 hours. Blend and pass to leave just the seeds behind and churn in an ice cream machine according to manufacturer's instructions.

to serve:
Serve the sorbet on the tapioca pudding in a glass.

chef's tip:
If fresh berries are not available, use 550g of frozen mixed berries.

PREPARATION TIME: 1½ HRS

COOKING TIME: 8 MINS

INGREDIENTS

apple purée:
(for the soufflé and the yoghurt)
1 kg pink lady apples
2 vanilla pods
2 cardamom pods
2 star anise
½ cinnamon stick

soufflé base:
100g sugar
500g purée, as above
40g cornflour

soufflé:
300g base, as above
180g whites
75g sugar

yoghurt:
10g sugar
25g apple purée, as above
100g Greek yoghurt

Spiced apple souffle with cinnamon flavoured greek yoghurt

BY JOHN WILLIAMS

INSTRUCTIONS

apple purée:
1. Quarter the apples, leaving the skin on and place in a large metal bowl with the vanilla pods, (scrape the seeds out by splitting in half and add both the pods and the seeds to the apples.)
2. Take the remaining spices and put them all into a muslin cloth and tie up in a bundle.
3. Add this to the apples and cling film the bowl.
4. Place on a large pan of simmering water and steam for approximately 1 hour or until the apples are soft and cooked.
5. Once cooked, remove the vanilla pods and muslin bundle, pass off excess fluid and blitz until smooth. Keep hot.

soufflé base:
1. Add the sugar to the purée and whilst whisking, bring to the boil.
2. When boiling, put the cornflour in a large bowl and add enough water to make a paste.
3. Add the boiling purée whilst whisking and then return the whole mix into the pan.
4. Bring the mix to the boil and cook out for approximately 3 minutes (until the flour taste has been cooked out).

soufflé:
1. To make 4 soufflés, ensure the base is very hot and in a separate clean bowl whisk the eggs whites and sugar to soft peak meringue.
2. Once at this stage, take one third of the meringue mix and add it to the base, whisking them together.
3. Once smooth take the other two thirds of the meringue and fold it in to the mix, ensuring light movements to maintain the air.
4. Pipe this mix into soufflé moulds that have been buttered and sugared, flatten with a palette knife and clean the edges.
5. Cook at 180°C for approximately 7 minutes.

yoghurt:

1. Take the sugar and bring to a slow caramel.
2. Once at a smooth golden colour, add a little purée and cook out, once this has combined add the remaining purée.
3. When cool, pass this mix and fold through Greek yoghurt to serve with the soufflé.

MAKES 4

PREPARATION TIME: 30 MINS +
CHILLING AND CHURNING TIME

COOKING TIME: 10 MINS

INGREDIENTS

12 fresh black figs
150g maple syrup
50g balsamic

Guinness ice cream:
220g Guinness
100g milk
100g cream
30g glucose
60g sugar
4 egg yolks

pistachio crumbs:
40g pistachios
65g plain flour
65g sugar
5g cornflour
40g melted butter

Figs, maple and balsamic, and Guinness ice cream

BY STEVE DRAKE

INSTRUCTIONS

1. Use only perfectly ripe black figs.
2. Cut into wedges and store on a tray in the fridge until needed
3. Mix the maple syrup and balsamic together in a bowl and whisk to fully incorporate. Store in the fridge until needed.

Guinness ice cream:
1. Pour the Guinness into a large bowl.
2. Boil the milk, cream and glucose.
3. Whisk the sugar and egg yolks until pale and pour on the cream mixture whilst whisking. Pour back into the pan and cook until it coats the back of a spoon.
4. Pass through a sieve onto the Guinness and chill for 2 hours.
5. Churn in an ice cream machine according to manufacturer's instructions and place in a tub in the deep freeze until needed.

pistachio crumbs:
1. In a food processor combine the pistachios and plain flour, mix until very fine.
2. Add the sugar and cornflour and slowly pour in the melted butter, it should have a breadcrumb-like texture.
3. Tip out onto a tray lined with greaseproof and bake at 150°C for 10 minutes. Halfway through turn over the mix with a fork to enable even cooking.
4. Allow to cool on the tray once cooked and store in a covered container in a cool place, but not the fridge.

to finish:
1. Take the figs out of the fridge 10 minutes before plating so they are at room temperature.
2. Place a tablespoon of pistachio crumbs in the middle of the plate and scatter the figs around.
3. Add a large spoon of ice cream and drizzle over the maple and balsamic syrup.

Sprinkle over salads

RED GRAPES

A good source of resveratrol

219

MAKES
20

PREPARATION TIME: 15 MINS

COOKING TIME: 12 MINS

Madeleines

BY JOHN WILLIAMS

INGREDIENTS

1 lemon, juice and zest
140g butter
50g milk
½ vanilla pod
250g flour
10g baking powder
4 whole eggs
200g sugar

INSTRUCTIONS

1. Bring the lemon juice and zest, butter, milk and vanilla to the boil and set aside.
2. Combine the flour and baking powder.
3. In a separate bowl, whisk the eggs and sugar and slowly add to the flour and baking powder to make a paste; add little by little, whisking from the middle to ensure no lumps form.
4. Pass the hot butter mix through a fine chinois and combine with the paste. Place in the fridge if not cooking the madeleines immediately. The mixture will keep for up to two days.
5. Heat the oven to 180°C, butter and flour a madeleine tin and pipe the mixture into the tin.
6. Cook for approximately 7 minutes, turn the tray and cook for a further 4 minutes or until risen and golden.
7. Dust with icing sugar to serve.

MAKES 4

PREPARATION TIME: 30 MINS

COOKING TIME: 15 MINS

Fruit parcels in filo pastry

BY DANIEL GALMICHE

INGREDIENTS

400g filo pastry sheets

plain flour, for dusting

60ml almond oil or flaxseed oil

310g mixed berries, or the fruit of
your choice, hulled and prepared as
necessary

2 vanilla pods, cut in half lengthways

4 petals of star anise

1 tsp freshly crushed black
peppercorns

3 tbsp caster sugar

zest 1 lime

icing sugar, for sprinkling

INSTRUCTIONS

1. Preheat the oven to 180°C. Unroll the filo pastry, spread it out on a lightly floured work surface and cut it into 16 rectangles, about 30x15cm. Brush each pastry rectangle with some of the oil, stacking one on top of the other to create 4 stacks of 4 pastry rectangles. By coating each piece of pastry in butter, you get a beautifully crumbly parcel. It also prevents the pastry from getting soggy when the fruit releases its juices during baking.

2. Leaving a 3cm wide border along the edges, arrange the fruit on a middle quarter of each pastry stack, keeping the remaining pastry free to fold over. Top each portion of fruit with half a vanilla pod and 1 star anise petal and sprinkle with the black pepper, sugar and lime zest.

3. Working with one pastry and fruit stack, position it horizontally on the work surface. Brush the edges of the pastry again with some of the remaining oil. Fold the right-hand side of the pastry over the fruit, then fold the left-hand side over to cover the pastry and fruit. Gently pinch the top and bottom open edges together and fold them under the parcel to make sure it is well sealed. Repeat until you have 4 individual parcels.

4. Transfer the parcels onto a greased baking sheet and sprinkle with icing sugar, which will create a lovely glaze during baking, Bake in the pre-heated oven for 15 minutes until golden brown and shiny. Serve warm.

MAKES 4

PREPARATION TIME: 20 MINS +
3 HRS FREEZING TIME

COOKING TIME: 15 MINS

Poached butternut squash with cranberry ice and grated chocolate

BY STEVE DRAKE

INGREDIENTS

poached butternut:
1 small butternut squash
1 vanilla pod
300g sugar
1 litre water
juice ½ a lemon

cranberry ice:
60g sugar
50g water
300g cranberry purée or juice

to serve:
50g dark chocolate, at least
    70% cocoa solids
mint

INSTRUCTIONS

poached butternut:
1. Peel and dice the butternut squash to a dice of approximately 2-3cm.
2. Place in a pan, in which it just covers the bottom and add the split vanilla pod, the sugar, water and juice of half a lemon.
3. Bring up to the boil and then simmer very gently for 15 minutes, being careful it doesn't break down.
4. Allow to cool in the pan and then refrigerate in a covered plastic container.

cranberry ice:
1. Dissolve the sugar in water and add the mixture to the cranberry purée.
2. Pour into a shallow plastic container and place in the freezer.
3. Once fully frozen, take a fork and scrape the frozen mixture to create snow like effect. Keep in the freezer until needed.

to serve:
1. Spoon the chunks of butternut into a shallow bowl adding a little juice.
2. Grate the chocolate over using the fine side. Tear a couple of mint leaves all over.
3. Sprinkle the cranberry ice/snow over and eat immediately.
4. For an extra flavour hit, a very small sprinkle of good instant coffee works very well.

MAKES 8-12

PREPARATION TIME: 1 HR

COOKING TIME: 1 HR +
2 HRS COOLING

INGREDIENTS

sponge:
125g soft butter
125g caster sugar
3 eggs beaten
125g self raising flour
zest and juice ½ orange

jelly:
3 leaves gelatine
250g raspberries
50g caster sugar
75ml white wine
75ml water

set custard:
2 leaves gelatine
275ml double cream
150ml full fat milk
½ vanilla pod
4 egg yolks
75g caster sugar
1 tbsp cornflour

to serve:
275ml double cream
splash sherry
hundreds and thousands

Summer trifle

BY GALTON BLACKISTON

INSTRUCTIONS

sponge:
1. Preheat the oven to 180°C.
2. In a bowl, cream together the butter and sugar until pale and creamy, then gradually add the eggs, a little at a time. Using a metal spoon, fold in the flour and add the orange zest and juice.
3. Pour the sponge mixture into a square cake tin, greased and lined with baking parchment. Bake in the oven for about 30 minutes until springy to the touch.
4. Remove from the oven and turn out onto a wire rack to cool. Once cooled slice into the terrine shape and press into a cling filmed lined terrine mould.

jelly:
1. Place the gelatine into a cold bath of water to soften.
2. Place the raspberries, sugar, white wine and 75ml of water in a pan.
3. Place on a medium heat and bring to the boil, after a few minutes remove from the heat and pass through muslin.
4. Place the juice back into the pan and bring back to the boil and stir in the gelatine leaves.
5. Allow to cool and as the juice starts to set, pour over the sponge. At this point you can if you want add a few strawberries or raspberries to the jelly. Place the terrine mould back in the fridge to set.

set custard:
1. Soak the gelatine leaves in cold water.
2. Place the cream and milk into a pan with the vanilla pod and bring to the boil.
3. In a bowl whisk together the egg yolks, sugar and cornflour until light and creamy.
4. Once the cream has come to the boil, remove from the heat and pour over the egg mixture. Whisk well and return to the heat, stirring continuously with a wooden spoon until the custard starts to thicken and coats the back of the spoon.

5. Stir in the gelatine leaves and remove from the heat, strain through a fine sieve and allow to cool slightly, at which point pour over the set jelly and cool until set.

to assemble the trifle:
1. Remove the trifle from the terrine mould and slice into generous portions.
2. Place 275ml of cream with a splash of sherry into a bowl and lightly whisk. Using a piping bag, pipe on top of your trifle and finish with some hundreds and thousands.

Rich in beta-carotene

PINEAPPLE

Tangy and sweet

SERVES
6

PREPARATION TIME: 40 MINS +
CHILLING TIME AS NECESSARY

Lemon posset with exotic fruits

BY JOHN WILLIAMS

INGREDIENTS

fruits:
1 kiwi
½ papaya
¼ pineapple
½ mango
1 passion fruit
2 limes, zested

posset:
175g sugar
575ml double cream
2 large lemons, zest and juice

INSTRUCTIONS

fruits:
Dice all to 5mm cubes. Add in the passion fruit seeds and lime zest and set aside.

posset:
1. In a pan, boil the sugar and cream.
2. Juice and zest the lemons and bring to the boil once the cream has come to heat.
3. Once both boiled, combine both mixtures together and pass through a fine chinois.
4. Pour into serving glass.
5. Refrigerate until set.
6. To serve, spoon the fruits onto the posset.

PREPARATION TIME: 15 MINS +
3 HRS COOLING TIME

Green tea and lime chocolate truffles

BY STEVE DRAKE

INGREDIENTS

100g double cream
4 green tea bags
420g Valrhona 40% milk chocolate
80g Valrhona 70% dark chocolate
2 limes, zested
10g honey
160g lime juice
60g unsalted butter, diced
3 tbsp cocoa powder

INSTRUCTIONS

1. Place the cream in a small saucepan and heat. When at boiling point add the tea, remove from the heat and infuse for 10 minutes.
2. Squeeze the tea bags between 2 spoons and discard.
3. Mix both chocolates together and melt in a metal bowl over some warm water.
4. Add the zest of the 2 limes to the chocolate.
5. Add the honey and lime juice to the cream.
6. Bring this liquid to the boil and pour onto the chocolate and stir using a whisk, until thoroughly incorporated.
7. Continue stirring, adding the diced butter a little at a time. Pour into a clean bowl and chill for 3 hours.
8. Using a large melon baller, scoop the chocolate and with your hands make into balls and chill until ready to use.

to finish:
Roll the chocolate in cocoa powder before serving.

Sauces & Vinaigrettes

SERVES
8

PREPARATION TIME: 5 MINS

Lime mayonnaise

BY GALTON BLACKISTON

INGREDIENTS

2 limes
1 egg
1 tsp English mustard powder
freshly ground pepper, for seasoning
275ml sunflower oil

INSTRUCTIONS

1. Zest 1 lime and set aside.
2. Juice both limes and place the egg, 2 tablespoons of lime juice and mustard powder in the bowl of a food processor, reserving the remaining juice for later use.
3. Season well, then whiz on a high speed until all the ingredients are combined.
4. Turn off the machine and, using a spatula, scrape down the sides of the bowl to make sure everything gets properly incorporated.
5. Turn the machine back on and very slowly drizzle in the sunflower oil; as you do so, the mixture will emulsify and gradually thicken. Add the grated lime zest and more juice if necessary.
6. Check the seasoning and transfer to the fridge until needed.

MAKES 600ML

Yoghurt dressing
BY PETER FIORI

PREPARATION TIME: 5 MINS

INGREDIENTS

2 egg yolks
1 tsp Dijon mustard
1 tbsp cider vinegar
150ml ground nut oil
75ml water
150ml yoghurt
4 tbsp hazelnut oil
3 tbsp chives, chopped

INSTRUCTIONS

1. Make the mayonnaise by whisking the egg yolks, Dijon mustard and cider vinegar.

2. Whisk in the ground nut oil slowly to emulsify then let down with the water.

3. Whisk in the yoghurt and finish with the hazelnut oil and chives.

Spicy tomato dip
BY PETER FIORI

MAKES 600ML

PREPARATION TIME: **10 MINS**

INGREDIENTS

2 egg yolks
juice ½ lemon
250ml olive oil
2 tbsp sun-dried tomato oil
10 cherry tomatoes
100g sun-dried tomatoes
2 cloves garlic
2 tsp harissa paste
4 pinches black pepper

INSTRUCTIONS

1. Combine the egg yolks and lemon juice in a clean blender and turn onto a medium speed. Once the egg yolks are fully combined with the lemon juice, combine the olive oil and sun-dried tomato oil and begin to drizzle into the egg yolk mix. Add the oil very slowly to avoid the mayonnaise splitting.

2. Half way through adding the olive oil mix, stop the blender and scrape down the sides to ensure the whole mix is being emulsified. Turn the blender back on and slowly add the remaining oil.

3. In a clean blender, combine the cherry and sun-dried tomatoes with the garlic, harissa, pepper and blend until the mix is almost smooth.

4. Combine the mayonnaise and tomato paste in a blender and blend at full speed for 1 minute.

237

MAKES
300ML

PREPARATION TIME: 15 MINS

INGREDIENTS

low fat mayonnaise
1 tsp harissa
pinch paprika
juice ½ lemon
50g smoked piquillo peppers
pinch cayenne pepper
roasted garlic cloves

INSTRUCTIONS

1. In a blender, add the mayonnaise, harissa, paprika, lemon juice, smoked piquillo peppers, cayenne pepper and roasted garlic cloves.
2. Blend to create a pimento mayonnaise.

Pimento mayonnaise
BY PETER FIORI

Ginger dressing
BY ANDREW FAIRLIE

PREPARATION TIME: **5 MINS**

COOKING TIME: 5 mins

INGREDIENTS

ginger dressing:
50g grated palm sugar
2tbs fish sauce
2tbs grated fresh ginger

INSTRUCTIONS

1. Combine the ingredients in a small saucepan, bring to a boil, remove from the heat, strain and cool.
2. This dressing can be found on page 118 in Andrew Fairlie's grilled fillet of salmon with green apple salad, ginger and lime dressing.

MAKES: 300-500ML DEPENDING
ON SIZE OF SHALLOT

PREPARATION TIME: 10 MINS

COOKING TIME: 1 HR

INGREDIENTS

6 large banana shallots
olive oil to cover
100ml good sherry vinegar

INSTRUCTIONS

1. Using a food processor, peel and chop the shallots into a small dice.
2. Cover with the oil and cook over a very low heat stirring from time to time for about 1 hour.
3. Once caramelised and completely cooked add the vinegar, cool and reserve for later use

chef's tip:
It keeps very well in the fridge and is wonderful with all ingredients, meat, fish and vegetables.

Caramelised shallot vinaigrette
BY SAM MOODY

Citrus vinaigrette

BY PETER FIORI

MAKES 220ML

PREPARATION TIME: 15 MINS

INGREDIENTS

1 tbsp Dijon mustard
zest ½ orange
zest ½ lime
zest ½ lemon
2 tbsp orange juice
1 tbsp lemon juice
1 tbsp lime juice
2 tbs sherry vinegar
freshly ground black pepper,
    for seasoning
200ml ground nut oil
1 tsp shallot, finely chopped
1 tsp ginger, peeled and finely chopped
3 tbsp tomatoes, peeled and diced

INSTRUCTIONS

1. Mix the mustard with the orange, lime and lemon zest.
2. Add the orange, lemon and lime juice, followed by the sherry vinegar and season.
3. Slowly whisk in the ground nut oil.
4. Finally add the chopped shallot, ginger and diced tomatoes.

Smoothies

Smoothies and juices have an important role to play both during treatment and when recovering, as they offer an easy solution to maximise vitamin and mineral intake. However, it is important to avoid large portions of fruit-based smoothies as they can be extremely calorific and have a high sugar content – it is, after all, quite unnatural for us to eat 5-6 portions of fruit in one sitting. Although, the sugars contained within fruit are 'natural', when blended the fibrous outer walls of the plant cells are destroyed meaning the fructose is absorbed quickly from the gut and the whole fruit has moved from having a relatively low glycaemic index (GI) to becoming a high-GI smoothie. This will cause a peak in your blood sugar levels that could leave you feeling sluggish in a couple of hours.

Ways to counteract this are to either make a predominantly vegetable based smoothie which will naturally have a lower sugar content, or to add a protein source such as yoghurt, milk or ground nuts which will delay the absorption of the glucose and lower the GI of the drink.

All of the smoothies in this section have been designed to include a selection of cancer-protective ingredients. A good example of this is the fruit and nut smoothie on page 248 which includes brazil nuts, an excellent source of Selenium, a mineral integral to our immune function and the anti-oxidant compound, quercetin.

SERVES
2

PREPARATION TIME: 5 MINS

INGREDIENTS

2 large handfuls of spinach
2 frozen bananas
400ml almond milk
3 apples

INSTRUCTIONS

1. Freeze the bananas in a sandwich bag, after peeling. This is a great way if using up bananas that have browned.
2. Add all of the ingredients to a blender and mix thoroughly.
3. Loosen with a little extra almond milk if the mixture seems too thick.
4. Pour into a glass and serve.

Green banana shake
BY KELLY MCCABE

Watermelon juice

BY KELLY MCCABE

PREPARATION TIME: 5 MINS

INGREDIENTS

½ watermelon, cut into cubes.
6cm of peeled cucumber
Either a squirt of lime, fresh mint
leaves or 1 tsp of grated ginger
    to flavour
ice

INSTRUCTIONS

1. Add all of the ingredients, except the ice, to a blender and mix thoroughly.
2. Add the ice to the blender and blitz for 30 seconds more.
3. Pour into a glass and serve.

chef's tip:
This is perfect for people who lose the taste for water during and after their treatment and are looking for an alternative low-sugar refreshing drink.

SERVES
2

PREPARATION TIME: 5 MINS

INGREDIENTS

1 large ripe mango, peeled and sliced
250g low fat natural yoghurt

INSTRUCTIONS

1. Add all the mango and yoghurt to a blender and mix thoroughly.
2. Loosen with a little extra milk if the mixture seems too thick.
3. Pour into a glass and serve chilled.

Mango lassi
BY KELLY MCCABE

Blue beetroot

BY KELLY MCCABE

PREPARATION TIME: 5 MINS

INGREDIENTS

2 small raw beetroots, peeled
and sliced
1 large handful of spinach
2 handfuls of frozen blueberries
and raspberries
100ml of cranberry juice

INSTRUCTIONS

1. Add all of the ingredients to a blender and mix thoroughly.
2. Loosen with a little extra cranberry juice if the mixture seems too thick.
3. Pour into a glass and serve.

SERVES 2

PREPARATION TIME: 5 MINS

COOKING TIME: 5 MINS

Fruit and nut smoothie

BY PETER FIORI

INGREDIENTS

35g almonds
35g walnuts
35g Brazil nuts
35g hazelnuts
90g water
2 apples
50g raisins
50g frozen black fruits
   (use from freezer)
4tbsp low fat yoghurt

INSTRUCTIONS

1. Take all the nuts and water, cover and place into the microwave (900w) on full power for 2 minutes and then cool down.

2. Juice the apples, put into a blender. Add the chilled nuts, raisins, frozen fruits, yoghurt and blend .

chef's tip:
Make sure all the ingredients are chilled before blending.

Fruit salad smoothie
BY PETER FIORI

SERVES 3

PREPARATION TIME: 5 MINS

INGREDIENTS

2 apples
2 pears
½ celery
3cm piece of cucumber
85g baby spinach
small bunch watercress
½ avocado
4 ice cubes

INSTRUCTIONS

1. Juice the apples, pears, celery, cucumber, spinach and watercress.
2. Add the flesh of the avocado and ice cubes to the blender along with the juice.
3. Pour into a glass and serve.

chef's tip:
Make sure all the ingredients are chilled before juicing and blending.

SERVES 2

PREPARATION TIME: 10 MINS

Watermelon, celery and cucumber replenisher

BY SIMON BOYLE

INGREDIENTS

500g fresh ripe watermelon
250g cucumber, without skin
100g celery
1 tbsp lemon juice
3 sprigs fresh mint
1 tbsp crushed flax seed

INSTRUCTIONS

1. Cut the melon, cucumber and celery and put through a fruit and vegetable juicer (a food processor will do). Add the lemon juice
2. Mix together until combined.
3. Chop the mint fairly fine and add to the juice.
4. Pour into glasses and sprinkle with flax seed.

Mango smoothie

BY SAM MOODY

PREPARATION TIME: 10 MINS

INGREDIENTS

300g mango purée
200g crème fraîche
1 whole lime
20ml water
orange juice, to adjust consistency

INSTRUCTIONS

1. Place all ingredients into a blender and blend until it reaches the desired consistency.
2. Pour into glasses and serve.

PREPARATION TIME: **10 MINS**

Raspberry smoothie
BY SAM MOODY

INGREDIENTS

300g of raspberry purée
200g crème fraîche
1 whole lime
orange juice, to adjust consistency

INSTRUCTIONS

1. Place all ingredients into a blender and blend until it reaches the desired consistency.
2. Pour into glasses and serve.

Banana smoothie

BY SAM MOODY

SERVES
4

PREPARATION TIME: 10 MINS

INGREDIENTS

2 bananas
2 whole limes
500g crème fraîche
orange juice, to adjust consistency

INSTRUCTIONS

1. Place all ingredients into a blender and blend until it reaches the desired consistency.
2. Pour into glasses and serve.

SERVES 2-3

PREPARATION TIME: 10 MINS

Banana and blueberry smoothie

BY MARK JORDAN

INGREDIENTS

1 punnet of blueberries
2 bananas
1 vanilla pod, scraped
1pt soya cream

INSTRUCTIONS

1. Place the blueberries and 1 banana into a blender and purée with the scraped vanilla pod until nice and smooth; at this point add some soya milk until it reaches a desired consistency.

2. Rinse the blender and add the remaining banana and purée, adding some soya milk to reach desired consistency. Pour over the first purée so that you get a purple smoothie with a yellow smoothie on top.

3. Slice a few raw blueberries and arrange on top of the smoothie and serve straight away.

Sea-bream baked in sea salt crust, fresh fennel and orange salad

STAGE-BY-STAGE PROCESS:

BY DANIEL GALMICHE

INSTRUCTIONS

1. Line a baking tray with a layer of the salt mixture. Ensure that the layer is larger than the fillets.
2. Place a sheet of greaseproof paper on the top of the salt layer. Place a fillet on top of this.
3. The fillet should sit comfortably on the paper so that it does not touch the salt.
4. Cover the fillet with a second sheet of greaseproof paper.
5. Press firmly.
6. Cover completely with the remaining mix. Press down firmly around the fish.
7. When cooked, rest then break the crust.
8. Remove crust carefully and discard.
9. Remove top sheet of paper carefully.
10. Remove the fish to a warmed plate and lift the skin from one side.
11. Serve as shown.

Glossary

ARROWROOT
A starch extract of the root of a tropical plant native to the Americas called maranta. Used for thickening sauces, juices and syrups.

BABA GHANOUSH
A Middle Eastern dip similar to hummus but made with aubergine instead of chickpeas.

BOUQUET GARNI
A bundle of fresh herbs, usually thyme, parsley and bay leaf, used to add flavour to soups, stews, stocks and poaching liquids.

BOUILLON
In French cuisine, a clear thin broth made typically by simmering beef or chicken in water with seasonings.

BOIS BOUDRAN
A French sauce typically containing oil, vinegar, ketchup, Worcestershire sauce, mustard, shallots, herbs and pepper

CARTOUCHE
A piece of baking paper, grease paper or wax folded three times and cut to the size required. Used to line a baking tin or cover a pan.

CHINOIS
A conical sieve with an extremely fine mesh, used to strain custards, purées, soups and sauces, producing a very smooth texture.

DEGLAZE
Adding liquid to a pan such as stock or wine to loosen and dissolve food particles that are stuck to the bottom in order to make a sauce.

EN PAPILLOTTE
A method of cooking in which the food is put into a folded pouch or parcel and then baked.

FILO PASTRY
Paper-thin sheets of pastry commonly used in Greek, Eastern European and Middle Eastern cuisines.

GARAM MASALA
A blend of ground spices commonly used as a base in many North Indian and other South Asian cuisines.

GRANITA
A semi frozen dessert made from sugar, water and various flavourings.

GRENADINE
A commonly used bar syrup characterised by its sweet and sour flavour and red colour.

HARISSA
A hot, red pepper paste used in North African cooking.

HON DASHI
A broth or fish stock found in Japanese cuisine.

JULIENNE
The French term for the method of cutting vegetables into long, thin strips like matchsticks.

KOMBU
Edible seaweed from the kelp family eaten widely in East Asia.

LEMON VERBENA
A perennial shrub with lemon scented leaves used to add a lemon flavour to a variety of dishes and herbal teas.

MACHE BOUQUET
A type of salad leaf.

MANDOLINE
A cooking utensil used for fine slicing and cutting julienne.

PATA NEGRA HAM
A type of cured ham produced mostly in Spain from the Pata Negra (Black Iberian) pig.

PEDRO XIMENEZ BALSAMIC VINEGAR
A sweet and sour vinegar made from Pedro Ximenez grapes.

PEQUILLO PEPPER
A sweet, slightly piquant red pepper

PURÉE
1 To blend or strain cooked food until a thick consistency; 'blend until a purée'.
2 Food that has been blended or strained.

QUINOA
A grain-like crop grown mainly for its edible seeds.

RAMEKIN
A small individual circular, porcelain glass or earthenware oven-proof dish.

RAS EL HANOUT
A blend of spices from North Africa.

SAUTÉ
A form of dry-heat cooking that uses a very hot pan and a small amount of fat to quickly cook food while browning the surface.

SCRUMPET
A forcemeat that has been coated in breadcrumbs and deep fried.

SOUFFLÉ
A light, fluffy baked dish made with egg yolks and beaten egg.

SUMAC
A tangy, lemon tasting spice often used in Mediterranean and Middle Eastern cuisine.

SZECHUAN PEPPER
A common spice used in Asian cuisine that has lemony and peppery overtones. Known for producing the "mouth numbing" quality typical of the Sichuan province of China.

TERRINE
1 A vessel for cooking a forcemeat loaf.
2 A forcemeat loaf similar to paté.

XERES VINEGAR
Also known as sherry vinegar, it has the rich, nutty, flavour of a fortified wine, mainly used in marinades for grilling and salad dressings.

CONVERSION CHART WEIGHT
(SOLIDS)

¼oz	5g
½oz	10g
¾oz	20g
1oz	25g
1 ½oz	40g
2oz	50g
2 ½oz	60g
¾oz	75g
4oz	110g
4 ½oz	125g
5 ½oz	150g
6oz	175g
7oz (2 cups)	200g
8oz (½lb)	225g
9oz	250g
10oz	275g
10 ½oz (3 cups)	300g
12oz (¾lb)	350g
13oz	375g
14oz (4 cups)	400g
1lb	450g
1lb 8oz	700g (1/2 kg)
2lb	900g
3lb	1.35kg
3lb 5oz	1.5kg
4lb	1.8kg

VOLUME (LIQUIDS)

1 teaspoon (tsp)	5ml
1 dessertspoon	10ml
1 tablespoon (tbsp)	15 ml or ½fl oz
1 fl oz	30ml
1 ½ fl oz	40ml
2 fl oz	60ml
3 fl oz	75ml
3 ½ fl oz	100ml
4 fl oz	120ml
5 fl oz	150ml or ¼ pint (pt)
6 fl oz	175ml
7 fl oz	200ml
8 fl oz	240ml
9 fl oz	260ml
10 fl oz	275ml or ½ pint
11 fl oz	325ml
12 fl oz	350ml
13 fl oz	375ml
14 fl oz	400ml
15 fl oz	450ml or ¾ pint
16 fl oz	475ml
18 fl oz	500ml (½ litre)
19 fl oz	550ml
20 fl oz	600ml or 1 pint
1 ¼ pints	725ml
1 ½ pints	875ml

1 ¾ pints	1 litre
2 pints	1.2 litres
2 ½ pints	1.5 litres
3 pints	1.7 litres
3 ½ pints	2 litres
1 qt	950ml
2 qt	1 litre
3 qt	2.25 litres
4 qt	4.5 litres
5 qt	5.5 litres

LENGTH

¼ inch (")	5mm
½ inch	1cm
¾ inch	2cm
1 inch	2 ½cm
1 ¼ inches	3cm
1 ½ inches	4cm
2 inches	5cm
3 inches	7 ½cm
4 inches	10cm
6 inches	15cm
7 inches	18cm
8 inches	20cm
10 inches	25 ½cm
11 inches	28cm
12 inches	30cm

OVEN TEMPERATURES

Celsius*	Fahrenheit	Gas	Description
110ºC	225ºF	Gas Mark	¼ Cool
120ºC	250ºF	Gas Mark	½ Cool
140ºC	275ºF	Gas Mark 1	Very low
150ºC	300ºF	Gas Mark 2	Very low
170ºC	325ºF	Gas Mark 3	Low
180ºC	350ºF	Gas Mark 4	Moderate
190ºC	375ºF	Gas Mark 5	Moderate, Hot
200ºC	400ºF	Gas Mark 6	Hot
220ºC	425ºF	Gas Mark 7	Hot
230ºC	450ºF	Gas Mark 8	Very hot
240ºC	475ºF	Gas Mark 9	Very hot

* For fan assisted ovens, reduce temperatures by 20°C

TEMPERATURE CONVERSION: 0°C = 32°F

Salad of organic salmon with carrot, coconut and lime dressing **84**
Sea bream baked in sea salt, fennel salad with orange and lime **186**

LOBSTER
Lobster salad with sweet and sour dressing, mooli and ginger **102**

M
MACKEREL
Salad of baked mackerel, watermelon, beetroot and raspberry vinaigrette **108**
Seared mackerel with pomegranate and manuka honey dressing **80**

MADELEINES 220

MANGO
Garam masala chicken wrap with mango dip **110**
Mango lassi **246**
Mango smoothie **251**
Poached strawberries with mango sorbet **196**

MAYONNAISE
Grilled corn pimento mayonnaise **64**
Lime mayonnaise **235**
Pimento mayonnaise **238**
Poached Loch Duart salmon, black garlic mayonnaise, potato and capers **114**

MONKFISH
Chargrilled monkfish loin, Oriental broth, pak choi **146**

MUESLI
Bircher muesli **42**

MUSHROOM
Broccoli and Kombu soup with girolle mushrooms and Borage flowers **140**
Wild mushrooms and herb omelette **50**

MUTTON
Pulled mutton shepherd's pie **174**

N
NUTS
Almond panna cotta, apricots and sorbet **202**

Asparagus, French beans and sugar snap peas with orange and hazelnuts **112**
Camargue red rice and quinoa salad with pistachios, orange and rocket **124**
Cauliflower and hazelnut couscous **74**
Fruit and nut smoothie **248**
Roast pigeon with walnuts and pomegranate **164**

O
OMELETTE
Wild mushrooms and herb omelette **50**

ORANGE
Asparagus, French beans and sugar snap peas with orange and hazelnuts **112**
Camargue red rice and quinoa salad with pistachios, orange and rocket **124**
Sea bream baked in sea salt, fennel salad with orange and lime **186**
Stewed prunes with cinnamon and orange **38**

P
PANNA COTTA
Almond panna cotta, apricots and sorbet **202**

PATA NEGRA
Baked beans, pata negra, poached egg **52**

PEA
Asparagus, French beans and sugar snap peas with orange and hazelnuts **112**
Chilli and garlic peas **66**
Spiced split yellow pea soup **138**

PEPPER
Baked eggs with tomato, onions and sweet peppers **182**
Grilled corn pimento mayonnaise **64**
Pepperade salad **94**
Pimento mayonnaise **238**

PIGEON
Roast pigeon with walnuts and pomegranate **164**

PINEAPPLE
Grilled tuna with pineapple salsa in a honey and hempseed bap **90**
Spiced pineapple with coconut sorbet and candied ginger **204**

POMEGRANATE
Roast pigeon with walnuts and pomegranate **164**
Seared mackerel with pomegranate and manuka honey dressing **80**

POSSET
Lemon posset with exotic fruits **230**

PRAWN
Paella of chicken, squid and prawns **172**

PRUNE
Stewed prunes with cinnamon and orange **38**

Q
QUAIL
Roast quail with spiced vegetables **100**

QUINOA
Braised lamb neck tagine, quinoa and sweet potato **192**
Camargue red rice and quinoa salad with pistachios, orange and rocket **124**

R
RABBIT
Farm rabbit casserole with garlic and lemon **180**
Grilled loin of rabbit with pearl barley and sweetcorn risotto **162**
Rabbit scrumpets, tarragon and mixed spice, roast beetroot **76**

RADISH
Lobster salad with sweet and sour dressing, mooli and ginger **102**
Vietnamese vegetable roll **72**

RASPBERRY
Poached beef fillet with semi dried figs and raspberry vinaigrette **144**
Raspberry smoothie **249**
Salad of baked mackerel, watermelon, beetroot and raspberry vinaigrette **108**

RATATOUILLE
Roasted halibut steaks with summer ratatouille **152**

RECIPES FOR
Life

First published in 2013 by Chef Books.

Chef Books
Network House, 28 Ballmoor, Celtic Court
Buckingham MK18 1RQ, UK

www.chefmagazine.co.uk

ISBN 978-1-908202-17-8

Printed by C.T. Printing in China

AUTHOR & PUBLISHER:	PETER MARSHALL
MANAGING EDITOR:	SHIRLEY MARSHALL
EDITORIAL AND DIETARY CONSULTANT:	KELLY MCCABE
SUB EDITOR:	HELEN HOMES
COVER ART:	CATHERINE BLACK
PHOTOGRAPHY:	PETER MARSHALL
	JODI HINDS
DESIGNER:	PHILIP DONNELLY